Pinocchio

A new version of the story by Carlo Collodi

by

BRIAN WAY

With the collaboration of
Warren Jenkins and the Arena Theatre Company

LONDON – DENNIS DOBSON
80 KENSINGTON CHURCH ST. – LONDON W8

This version of **PINOCCHIO** is
DEDICATED
to
THE EDUCATIONAL DRAMA ASSOCIATION

First published in 1954
Second impression 1963
Third impression 1966
Fourth impression 1968
Fifth impression 1971

Permission to produce this play must be obtained from:
Dobson Books Ltd., 80 Kensington Church Street,
London, W8

ROYALTIES: *Amateur and School Production* £ 4 0 0 for every
performance.

*Professional or Children's Theatre, Radio or T.V.
Productions* by arrangement with the publishers.

SBN 234 77342 1

Published in Great Britain by Dobson Books Ltd.
Printed in Great Britain by A. Wheaton & Co.
Exeter, Devon

FOREWORD
by PETER SLADE

It is a great honour to be asked to write a foreword to this play, for it is a milestone in theatrical history. Brian Way is one of the few professionals who have been able to spend years studying children, and talking to education specialists about them. Faced with a particular issue, he does not retreat out of loyalty for adult theatre, but changes his position in favour of the needs of the child. This takes courage. But it is the only thing for genuine Children's Theatre writers to do. Because Mr Way has done it, we have received from his hand a play, which is as charming in its innocence as it is believable in performance.

The form of his play accepts in full the educational truth that many of us have known for years, that healthy minded children need and love to be up and doing. If grown-ups wish to act before children (or older children to younger ones), this must be taken into account, and the best performances in future will use purposeful passages of time in which children can be part of the show. This is logical, for if the actors succeed in creating a believable situation, then the little mind watching believes implicitly, and a real situation with real characters means talking to those characters and helping them on part of their journey through life. That is what makes children rise from their seats and cry out at exciting films. But many adults weep on their chocolate in the cigaretty cloud of dark. Is not the truth that we all want to help our friends through life? We sympathise, because we experience, or have experienced, the same things, or know that they could be so. Sympathy is self-identification. This Pinocchio is the simple real "it's ME" that every child will recognise, from his earliest attempts at living and walking, through his troubles, to the end. This play shows each living member of the audience a simple consideration of life itself, and makes possible a healthy and proper participation by all the little Pinocchios in that place; be they birds, beasts or just friends, they are by now all part of Pinocchio. If the actors will believe what they act, and not act down to their audience, and if they train themselves to be sensitive to the suspension of adult theatre timing, whilst participation is taking place, this play will prove of exceptional educational value. Older children will also be able to play it well for their own or others' joy, but it is in particular a golden barge for smooth conveyance by sympathetic adults, to a profound experience of reality, despite the fact that its story lies in the Land of Dreams.

Birmingham, September 22, 1953.

INTRODUCTION

Pinocchio was written for production in arena theatre. This is because it is not a play for children merely to *watch*, but one in which they could and should *participate*. Arena theatre is admirably suited to true and genuine participation, which is so much more than several hundred children "raising the roof" with a familiar song or with shouted replies to members of the cast. It means *sharing* the production —even, if we are able to take it all the way, *sharing* in the creation of the play.

It is not easy to participate in most of our proscenium theatres. There is a gulf between actor and audience, partly physical and partly spiritual, that makes it impossible for true sharing to take place. Arena theatre has no such gulf; the keynote is intimacy out of which participation begins to be possible. This was the inevitable conclusion drawn from the experiments of the West Country Children's Theatre Company, confirmed and furthered by the experiments conducted over a much longer period by Peter Slade, and now acknowledged by many other people.

* * * * *

Present-day professionalism will always be an obstacle to such a Children's Theatre. Economic considerations demand capacity houses, involving large audiences, and the presence of many adults. Tradition demands spectacle and finished artistry which destroy participation by offering a thing to be *watched* rather than in which to *take part*. The artists are produced to the last flicker of an eyelid so removing almost any possibility of a flexible reaction to the response of any audience. In true Children's Theatre there is need for a minimum of material show from the actors and the maximum of flexibility.

* * * * *

Most of our professional actors are not trained to be flexible; for this reason and because children today do not expect to be allowed to participate in a theatre, it was necessary, in the first instance, to plan each step in the development of audience participation. It was also necessary to give the cast practice in improvisation in the hope that they would be flexible enough not to reject a response from the audience once it came. This training took the form of improvisation round the story of the play; certain scenes were left unscripted for the actors to build up in rehearsal through improvisation. These features of the play have been retained in this published script, which is, for the most part, the same as the first script before production, with the addition of three scenes and the alteration (one hopes improvement) of some others. Flexibility remains a primary need for any other groups of actors attempting the play.

Ideally, this flexibility should be such that not only can the plot be changed according to suggestions from the audience (see production Note N in Act 2) but also that every line could be changed, the new lines being said with the conviction and polish of thorough rehearsal. For example, in the breakfasting scene early in Act 2, Pinocchio, in rehearsal, may have mimed cooking sausages. But if he asks the audience what *they* want for breakfast, they may reply "eggs" or even "kippers". It would break the whole bond with them if Pinocchio then still insisted on "sausages" and they would naturally be less eager to help him subsequently as they will find it difficult to believe that he will accept that help. Participation thus builds up slowly by attention to small details rather than broad effects. Six hundred children shouting hysterically does not necessarily mean that participation is taking place; one child running forward with a cloth for an over-eaten actor to wipe his mouth may mean that it is. The sensitive actor knows, and behaves accordingly.

*   *   *   *   *

Pinocchio offers wide scope to a group, composed either of adults or of senior children, who have only the floor space of a school hall and some ingenuity. The play could be performed with hats, scarves and other tokens rather than complete costumes. There can be such exciting drama under these conditions.

But adults attempting it for children may perhaps need to consider a reorientation of view of audiences for Children's Theatre; no longer should it be "how many can we get in to do our show *at*", but "what is the best way of sharing this play with the people who come to see it?" This may mean fewer people at each performance but it also means that more people may have an unforgettable experience. Which, in the long run, is more important?

*   *   *   *   *

Some will notice that the original story by Collodi has not been followed very closely. This is because it was not really a very pleasant story. Walt Disney also found this out and made many changes himself, which are his own copyright and are absent from this play which is after all *our* story of Pinocchio, the puppet who after many adventures became a boy. That is how we want each producing group and each audience to feel . . . it is also *their* story!

Acknowledgements are specially due to John English and Alicia Randle, governing director and general manager respectively of the Arena Theatre Company. They had the initiative to seek a really good new play for children, one that was really *for* children. They were rewarded by delighted audiences and what the Northern Critic of the *News Chronicle* called 'the best new children's play for years'. Warren Jenkins directed the first production and in doing so took a very full and important part with John English and Brian Way in many script conferences and in the development of the story. Finally and particularly we must mention the first company of actors listed on another page who met all the novelty of treatment and method, the difficulty of giving the first week's performance in the expanse of a large summer theatre where it was terribly hard even under the best conditions, to create an intimate atmosphere so desirable for such a children's play. They received their reward in the enthusiasm and whole-hearted co-operation of both young and old in every one of their audiences.

*   *   *   *   *

The action of the play takes place in and around Gepetto's house in a small Italian village.

The play is presented in three parts with two intervals.

The play was first proauced by the Arena Theatre
Company at Catlin's Arcadia, Llandudno, on the 29th
December, 1951 (and subsequently at the Library
Theatre, Manchester, the Arena Theatre, Newcastle-
upon-Tyne, Hanley, Walsall, Macclesfield, Wallasey,
Keighley, Birmingham, Cardiff and Weston-super-
mare) with the following cast:

Fire-Eater (a Puppet Showman)	Norman Welsh
Harlequin ⎫	Bernard Hepton
Columbine ⎬ 3 Puppets	Shirley Pannell
Pantalone ⎭	Kendrick Owen
Candlewick (Fire-Eater's Son) . . .	Jonathan Meddings
	Diana Chadwick
Ticket Sellers . . . . . . ⎨	Helen Lindsay
	Jennifer Stuart
Gepetto (a Puppet Maker)	Howard Goorney
Fairy	Elizabeth Orion
Antonio	Nigel Ince
Pinocchio (a Puppet)	David Stevens
Policeman	Bill Matthews
Fox (a Shady Gentleman) . . .	Kendrick Owen
Cat (his Follower)	Jonathan Meddings
1st Detective	Howard Goorney
2nd Detective	Bernard Hepton
1st Bloodhound	Diana Chadwick
2nd Bloodhound	David Marsden
Coachman	Kendrick Owen
Circus Master	Bernard Hepton
Donkey Girl	Jennifer Stuart
Clown	David Marsden
Acrobat	Diana Chadwick
Snake Charmer	Helen Lindsay
Maid	Diana Chadwick

The play produced by WARREN JENKINS
Assisted by BRIAN WAY
Decor by RICHARD LAKE
Costumes by MASQUERADE
Stage Director: JOHN FRANKAU
Dances arranged by ROSALIE WILLIAMS
Stage Manager: BILL MATTHEWS
Assistant Stage Managers: DAVID MARSDEN
and JENNIFER STUART

THE ARENA THEATRE COMPANY LIMITED
1951–2 Season

Governing Director . . .	John English
General Manager . . .	Alicia Randle
Director of Productions . .	Warren Jenkins
Public Relations Officer .	Andrew Campbell

CAST OF CHARACTERS

Note: In a fluid production, the order of appearance will
probably not be adhered to. The only characters which
cannot be doubled are GEPETTO, the FAIRY in her various
disguises, PINOCCHIO, and the CLOWN who can find so
much to do as himself.

In this version of the play, the CLOWN is an interesting example of a whole *character* that can be built up
during the production, with only the barest outline to
go on. In the Arena Theatre's production, Warren
Jenkins built up the part until it was almost the
'biggest' in the play. But no details have been recorded
here, simply because those details belong to *that* production and *that* actor. Each actor and producer
should together build their own ideas. But perhaps
one word of warning should be given. The humour
of the clown is not simply 'mucking about'—
it comes from sincere, absorbed *doing;* because he is
the clown he nearly always *does* in the wrong manner
or is in someone's way. But it is nevertheless serious.

PRODUCTION NOTES.

These notes will not answer all your problems. They are suggestions: much of the value in the production lies in working out one's own answers. Brian Way will always be interested to hear how different companies have tackled the play. He will help with advice wherever possible, and would appreciate an invitation to attend any production at which adults are allowed to be present.

Groups who have never attempted this kind of theatre before would also obtain advice from the Educational Drama Association, which has undertaken continual research into all kinds of Children's Theatre for many years.

(1) This, of course, can be anywhere, according to the shape of production.

(2) This 'moment of opening' will vary with each performance. Only Gepetto can decide the *right* moment for each different audience.

(3) Though scripted with a ticket-seller, Gepetto might well have similar conversations with members of the audience as he is trying to get at the ticket-seller.

(4) A clown, with large drum, should be an important member of Fire-Eater's Company, supplying much genuine comedy. In the original production he appeared as a mime throughout, speaking not one word. He was very helpful with the various placards and properties.

NOTES ON AUDIENCE PARTICIPATION.

NOTE The object here is to start participation with something of a
A shock, stating, in capitals as it were, that this is not to be a play at which one sits comfortably watching in one direction; things happen in every area; people journey in every direction. Included in the opening could be the dusting and arranging of the puppets, with members of the audience being invited to help.

B In cases of productions that take place partly on proscenium stages, it is often wise to show that the actors are not going to remain solely on the stage; hence Gepetto might enter *on* the stage and later come away from it and into the audience area. (There is a difference between the significance of this movement and that of the actors who, at the beginning of the play, come from all parts of the hall.)

C The other 'actors' could, if wanted, guide attention to Gepetto during this conversation—by their own interest in him and not by words of command.

Act I

On the stage area (1) we see Gepetto's house and the house and workshop of Fire-Eater, the Puppet showman.

About five minutes before the advertised time of the performance, as many of the company as can be spared mingle with the audience selling tickets or programmes for the 'Great Fire-Eater's Puppet Show'. Some of them have boards announcing that the show can be seen 'in this city' in three days' time.

    NOTE A.

A few minutes later (i.e. just prior to opening of play itself) GEPETTO *the puppet-maker, comes from his house (stage area) and stands listening to the ticket-sellers, etc. He moves down into the auditorium and 'fights' his way through to one of the ticket-sellers (2).*

    NOTE B.

GEPETTO   Did you say tickets for the puppet show——? (3)

TICKET S.   That's right, sir. The greatest puppet show on earth.

GEPETTO   Oh, yes, yes, yes, I know—it's wonderful. Wonderful. But—is it tonight——?

TICKET S.   Well, sir, there's a short performance tonight—just a sample of what you can look forward to at the big show in three days' time.

GEPETTO   I see. Then please may I have the best seat you've got for sixpence. I can't afford more than sixpence I'm afraid.

TICKET S.   Never mind—here you are, sir. [*he gives ticket*]

GEPETTO   Thank you. Thank you very much.

TICKET S.   You're welcome, sir. Excuse me asking, sir, but aren't you Mr Gepetto, the puppet-maker?

GEPETTO   Yes, yes, I am.

TICKET S.   I thought I recognised you, sir. Well, do stay and see the preview—it starts in a few minutes.

GEPETTO   Thank you, I will.

                [*Much of this may not be heard by many in the audience—but no matter (certainly no straining) as all the main details will come out later.*

                    NOTE C.

                Either the PUPPET THEATRE (*made of two painters' ladders with trestle boards across the top*) *will already be set up on the stage area, or else* FIRE-EATER *will come on to the area, clap his hands, and call for the setting up to be done at this point (i.e. after Gepetto's conversation with the Ticket Seller). Then the puppets* PANTALONE, HARLEQUIN *and* COLUMBINE *are set up in front of the trestle, and the three manipulators climb on to the trestle.* (4)

(5)   For central staging or a constantly fluctuating area of playing space, houselights might remain on throughout. They might, of course, be the only lighting available.

D   Well into the audience area would be best. After the first 'explosion', participation will be built slowly. In Act I, the main responsibility for this rests with Gepetto, who should build a strong bond with the audience. (Later it will be seen that this main responsibility is passed from Gepetto to Pinocchio.)

E   This music will perhaps always be canned. But it would be interesting if someone were to try making their own music with their own instruments—gongs, drums, tins, bells, needles in tins and so on.

F   The beginnings of participation between one member of the cast and the audience. N.B.: He *shares* his thoughts—ever ready to take up answers from the audience.

If possible, GEPETTO *should have a seat in front of the audience. If not, he can sit on the edge of one side of the stage.*

NOTE D.

When all are seated, FIRE-EATER *climbs on to stage. The house lights remain on during his talk.*] (5)

FIRE-EATER   Ladies and Gentlemen, Boys and Girls. It's very nice to see you all here today, and I hope you're all comfortable because it's just about time to see my puppets. But what you are about to see is only a sample of the big show you will be able to see in three days' time—tonight (this afternoon) you will see just one short dance by three of my finest puppets —Harlequin, Columbine and Pantalone. But if you come back at the end of the week you'll see a long, long show, with many, many more people in it. So— music please.

[*There is music.*

NOTE E.

We see a short and amusing dance-mime between HARLEQUIN, COLUMBINE *and* PANTALONE *as puppets operated by the manipulators. It is almost a 'trailer' of (indeed a section of) the Harlequinade that will take place at the end of Act 3.*

GEPETTO *leads the applause at the end of the dance.* FIRE-EATER *returns, and with the puppets and their manipulators, acknowledges the applause. The puppets and the theatre are then 'taken down' and out. They must not be taken back into the* FIRE-EATER'S *House as, in effect, they are going off to do the 'trailer' in other parts of the town.*]

FIRE-EATER   Thank you. Thank you. And that, my friends, is just a sample. There's much more to it than that. I'll let you into a secret—Pantalone is very fond of sausages, and you can imagine the fun when the clown pinches the sausages and skips with them.

[*He goes into peals of merriment as the clown demonstrates this.*]

Oh, ho, it makes me split my sides every time. Well, we must be off to show other people what to expect. Good-bye for now, everyone. Good-bye.

[*Music.* FIRE-EATER *and his troupe exit.*

As the music fades away, GEPETTO *comes a little more on to the apron and sits again. He has been very moved by the performance, and shares his thoughts with us.*]

NOTE F.

GEPETTO   Well, well, well, well. Upon my soul. Just think of it. Wasn't it wonderful? Simply beautiful. You know—

15

I make puppets. Lots of them. Some of them for Mr Fire-Eater. As a matter of fact I made those three—the ones you've just seen—for him. Hmmm, but that was some time ago. I have such a lot of fun making them. And yet, d'you know what I've always really wanted to do? I've always wanted to make a puppet that could walk without any strings at all! Yes, yes. Think of it. Me, a poor old man— what fun I'd have! Sometimes you know I want it so much that I sit and wish very hard with my eyes shut like this [*he demonstrates*]. But it doesn't seem to work. I suppose the trouble is that I'm so little that I can't wish big enough. Eh? Could be that, you know. Ooooooh! Ooooh! Wait a minute though. Ooooh, I,—I don't want to trouble *you*, you know, but—but perhaps you'd like to help. Course nothing might happen—but then again something might— if we wished hard ALL TOGETHER. [*whispering*] Shall we try it? Shall we? Oh, thank you, thank you very much. Well, let's all close our eyes and wish, and wish, and wish, very, very hard. If only one of us so much as peeps out of the corner of one eye—then it mightn't work. So now, let's try it. Close your eyes and wish—and wish—and wish— and wish——

> [*Slowly from the distance is heard 'charmingly eerie music'. The* FAIRY *comes from the audience area to stand behind* GEPETTO. *She is not a Christmas-tree Fairy. She is puckish, humorous, constantly busy, always either appearing or disappearing, constantly changing character, thus becoming all the people who subsequently help Pinocchio out of his difficulties (e.g. Cricket, the Frog, the Bird, and the Tight-rope Walker). For this first entrance she is* herself *and on her dignity—but it is a nice dignity, and there is a sort of 'mystery' about her that makes us want to see her again.*
> *Gently she touches* GEPETTO.
> *A gong or cymbals announce the fulfilment of the wish.*] (6)

NOTES

(6) Important. This was not done in the first performances with the result that some youngsters are still wishing with their eyes shut.

(7) This could be through the audience area, and Gepetto could enlist the support of the audience to listen for the noise of sawing and to guide him to where it comes from.   (See page 17.)

GEPETTO	Sssssssh—please—sssssh. In a moment. You see—we're all wishing very hard. Shhhhhhhh.
FAIRY	Well, you can stop wishing now, Mr Gepetto.
GEPETTO	Stop? Why?
FAIRY	Because I've come in answer to your wish.
GEPETTO	You?
FAIRY	Yes. I heard you and came at once.
GEPETTO	Oh, I say. Well, that's very nice of you. Might I ask—ask who you are?
FAIRY	I haven't got a name.
GEPETTO	No name?
FAIRY	No. Sorry. You see I'm so many people that I need so many names that I'd never remember them all.
GEPETTO	No. I suppose not. But why are you so many people?
FAIRY	I don't think I'd better tell you that. You'll find out in time. Sometimes it's very useful, you know.
GEPETTO	Yes, I suppose it must be.
FAIRY	Now tell me. Why did you want to see me?
GEPETTO	Well, I didn't exactly want to see *you*.
FAIRY	No, of course not. Then why were you wishing so hard?
GEPETTO	Oh, that. That was because I've always thought how wonderful it would be to make a puppet—I'm a puppet-maker, you know—to make a puppet that could move without strings! That's what we were wishing for when—when you came.
FAIRY	Tell me, Mr Gepetto. Do you know Antonio's yard?
GEPETTO	Of course I do. It's not very far from here. I always buy my logs from him.
FAIRY	He's busy cutting a very special log now. Listen! [*in distance, sound of sawing*] D'you hear?
GEPETTO	Yes.
FAIRY	Go to Antonio and ask him for that log.
GEPETTO	But——
FAIRY	Don't ask why, Mr Gepetto, or he may sell it to someone else before you get there.
GEPETTO	Oh dear, then I'd better hurry. Goodbye and thank you very much.
	[*He runs right from stage area—stops, turns to call goodbye again, but the* FAIRY *is hiding*.]
GEPETTO	[*to audience*] Thank you very much for helping me wish. It did work, didn't it?
	[*Then, muttering about the wonder of it all, he makes his way to* ANTONIO's *yard. When within 'hailing' distance, he stops*.] (7) (See page 16.)
GEPETTO	Not far now. Listen. You can hear his sawing quite clearly from here. [*calling*] Mr Antonio. Mr Antonio.
	[*Sawing continues, then stops*.]

B

ANTONIO	[*off*] Halloa! Who's there?
GEPETTO	It's me. Gepetto.
ANTONIO	Coming. Won't be a moment.
	[*Sawing continues.*]
GEPETTO	Oh, Mr Antonio.
ANTONIO	I won't be a moment, I say.
	[*The sawing 'completes its job'.* ANTONIO's *footsteps are heard.*]
ANTONIO	[*still off*] Where are you?
GEPETTO	I'm here, Mr Antonio.
ANTONIO	[*appearing*] Ah, there you are. Well, well, you are an impatient old codger this morning. What's the matter?
GEPETTO	Nothing's the matter. Really. All I want is a log.
ANTONIO	To make another puppet, eh?
GEPETTO	Yes, yes. A very special puppet.
ANTONIO	Well, let's go and see what we can find.
GEPETTO	No, no, please. Please. I would like to have the log you've just finished sawing.
ANTONIO	Would you indeed? And what's wrong with the rest of my timber, may I ask?
GEPETTO	Oh, nothing, nothing, really. It's just that—oh dear, I can't explain it to you. You must please believe me. It's terribly important that I have that log.
ANTONIO	My, you are in a state. Well, I suppose there's no reason why you shouldn't. Not so far to carry it anyway.
GEPETTO	Oh, thank you, thank you.
ANTONIO	When will you pay me for it?
GEPETTO	Next time I've earned some money. Very soon, I hope.
ANTONIO	All right. I'll give you a hand over with it. Come on— it's just by the gate.
	[*They disappear; the* FAIRY *comes from hiding and fills the place with magic. She hides again as the men re-appear carrying a heavy log. They put it down just outside* GEPETTO's *house.*]
GEPETTO	Just down here, please. There. Thank you very much.
ANTONIO	Not a bit. And all the best with your new puppet——
GEPETTO	Thank you——
ANTONIO	And don't forget you owe me tenpence halfpenny——
GEPETTO	I won't, I won't——
ANTONIO	Good day——
GEPETTO	Good day, Mr Antonio.
	[*As* ANTONIO *is moving away, we hear, from the distance, the 'charmingly eerie music'.*]
ANTONIO	Funny.
GEPETTO	What is?
ANTONIO	Do you hear noises?
GEPETTO	Noises? What sort of noises?
ANTONIO	Well, sort of queer music.

	[GEPETTO *listens—he hears it and recognises it as being the return of the* FAIRY. *But he doesn't want* ANTONIO *to know, so he indicates to the audience that they mustn't say anything.*]
ANTONIO	There it is again—don't you hear it?
GEPETTO	Oh yes, I hear it now.
ANTONIO	Do you? What is it, Mr Gepetto?
GEPETTO	I think it's the wind in the tree tops, Mr Antonio.
ANTONIO	So it is. Well, fancy that now. And I've never noticed it before.

[*And he goes out. When he's gone,* GEPETTO *listens very carefully—the music is still there.*]

GEPETTO [*to audience*] I wonder what it means. (8) [*he looks round*] She must be somewhere about. [*continues searching*] Can't see her anywhere though. Never mind—perhaps she'd rather I didn't see her. The best thing I can do is to sharpen the chisels ready to make my new puppet.

[*He sets eagerly to work away from the log. As soon as his back is turned, the* FAIRY *appears again, still as herself, but now looking really full of tricks. She weaves a spell over the log—not a 'wand' spell, but more of a puckish hypnotic movement. She draws, as it were, where the details of the face will come—and then breathes life into the log. She hides again, and* GEPETTO *comes and repeats the outline of the face. He hits once with the chisel and there is a flash and a puff of smoke.* GEPETTO *dashes through it to the front of stage area, to audience.*] (9)

GEPETTO Good Heavens! Did I do that?

[*He turns, and as the smoke clears away, we see, instead of a log, the completed puppet lying motionless on its back.* GEPETTO *moves toward it, looks at it from all sides, and then comes back to the audience.*]

NOTES

(8) He could enlist the support of the audience again here by asking if they have seen the Fairy, who, in her turn, can convey to them that she doesn't want them to tell. All these things help to build participation. Important, though, not just to get people shouting—good training for the cast.

(9) Each group will find its own way of mastering the technicalities involved in the birth of the puppet.

GEPETTO   That was quick, wasn't it? My chisel hardly touched it.

> [*He returns and looks again at the puppet, mumbling about how nice it is.* (10) *Then, suddenly, he has a thought and returns to the audience.*]

GEPETTO   Oh dear—I've forgotten something. I haven't thought of a name for him. Oh dear, how difficult it is. Now what should I call him d'you think? What was that? Pinocchio? Pinocchio! Well, that sounds nice—I think. Pinocchio! Pinocchio! Yes, yes. I like that. Wonder what he'll think of it. (11)

PINOCCHIO   It's all right.

> [GEPETTO *freezes—with his back to* PINOCCHIO.]

GEPETTO   Did you—did you—hear—that? It—it—he spoke. Didn't he? My puppet. He spoke. Oh, how wonderful. It's come true. My wish—it's come true. Or did I imagine it? I'll try again.

> [*He tiptoes towards* PINOCCHIO—*is about to speak— then can't bring himself to, so tiptoes back to the audience.*]

GEPETTO   Oh dear, I don't like to try again. I mean just suppose I *had* only imagined it? Hmmm? Still, I must find out sometime. Oh! I know.

> [*He screws his face up and puts his hands over it.*]

GEPETTO   [*in half whisper*] Pin—Pinocchio! Pinochiooo! (12)

PINOCCHIO   Hello. Where are you?

NOTES

(10) In a sense Gepetto has given birth to this object—hence his feelings toward it should be very personal to himself. These will differ with all Gepetto's so no attempt is made to put dialogue in for the words 'mumbling'.

(11) By now, if any kind of a bond has been built, the audience will readily suggest the name 'Pinocchio'. But any other names suggested should be taken equally seriously, and perhaps be turned down on the grounds of wanting a special name for so special a puppet.

(12) He might ask audience to help call this time—but it is not an enormous yell that's required.

GEPETTO	It is. It is true. [*he runs to* PINOCCHIO] Here I am, Pinocchio. Here I am.
PINOCCHIO	What's Pinocchio?
GEPETTO	Your name.
PINOCCHIO	Oh. What's yours?
GEPETTO	Gepetto.
PINOCCHIO	Gepetto! Oh, well why can't I be called Gepetto, too?
GEPETTO	Well, that would be a bit confusing, wouldn't it?
PINOCCHIO	Yes, I suppose it would. Well, aren't you going to help me up? I'm getting a bit stiff lying here.
GEPETTO	Oh, I'm sorry. I was so excited, I forgot. Of course I'll help you up. Now, up you come—urrrp—there—right—up—on—your—feet. [*He gets* PINOCCHIO *right up on his feet—then he takes his arms away and* PINOCCHIO *drops in a heap.* GEPETTO *runs to his aid.*]
GEPETTO	Oh dear, oh dear, oh dear. Oh, don't tell me you've got to have strings like all the others. Oh, I had so hoped——
PINOCCHIO	Strings. What strings?
GEPETTO	Well, you see, most puppets work by strings—but I hoped you'd be able to manage without.
PINOCCHIO	And I shall. Come on, give me a hand. It's only a matter of practice—isn't it?
GEPETTO	Yes. I suppose it is.

NOTES

G   This whole sequence will be different in detail with each Gepetto and Pinocchio—it is impossible to script such a scene for the satisfaction of every pair. Pinocchio is about to master certain skills—and this is always of some genuine amusement to any watchers who have already mastered them. Sincere effort to learn by him, and to teach by Gepetto will bring the humour in, thus avoiding the necessity of trying hard to be funny.

[*The dialogue for the next episode can be built up during rehearsals. Gradually* PINOCCHIO *masters first* balancing *on his own, then step by step* walking, *and then* running. *Finally he is so carried away by the excitement of it all, and by* GEPETTO's *enthusiasm, that he runs among the audience (sharing the delight of these new wonders), with* GEPETTO *calling to him to be careful; eventually* PINOCCHIO *runs right out at the back of the auditorium.* GEPETTO *is about to follow when he hears the 'eerie music' again, and a* CRICKET *(again the Fairy) appears behind him.*]

NOTE G.

CRICKET   Don't worry, Mr Gepetto. He'll be back.

GEPETTO   Yes. Yes. But he might fall over or something. He might even—hello, who are you?

CRICKET   Cricket.

GEPETTO   Oh. How do you do. Where d'you come from?

CRICKET   Oh, I was just running by, you know. Thought I'd look in and see how everything is.

GEPETTO   But——

CRICKET   I'm glad you got to Antonio's in time—for the log, I mean.

GEPETTO   Good gracious me. You're not a Cricket at all.

CRICKET   I most certainly am.

GEPETTO   Yes, yes, I know. But you're really the—the person who came after we had wished very hard.

CRICKET   Perhaps. Perhaps not.

GEPETTO   Oh, I understand. You don't want me to talk about it?

CRICKET   Some things are best not talked about. Anyway, I'm glad to see that it's all happened as you hoped.

GEPETTO   Yes, it has. Thank you very much. It's—— It's wonderful.

CRICKET   And now you have a puppet that can move without strings.

GEPETTO   Yes, isn't it exciting?

CRICKET   How would you like him to become a real boy, one day?

GEPETTO   A real boy? A real boy? But—— I can't believe it.

CRICKET   It might happen. You never know.

GEPETTO   A real boy. Like having a son of my own.

CRICKET   Now you mustn't get too excited, Mr Gepetto. It won't happen for a long time. Pinocchio's got a lot to learn. It'll be some time before he's ready to be a boy. And another thing——

GEPETTO   Yes?

CRICKET   You must take good care of him, Mr Gepetto. Everything will be very new to him, and if he goes off having adventures, you mustn't worry, I'll keep an eye on him.

23

H   This is the first of many *chases* through the audience, confirming yet again that all 'the theatre' is the scene of action. It is also an opportunity for the actors to test those parts of the audience that should be gently approached because of any very young or sensitive children—the action should flow past these. Training in group sensitivity among the cast becomes of great importance so that anyone who happens to shoot into one of the gangways can be 'missed' without any cessation or change in the flow of movement.

(13)   In all these cases, the improvised dialogue must be as real as the learned parts of the script, not just mumbled 'filling in'. This means hard practice at improvisation.

(14)   This word has very much the significance a loud drum beat would have in the same place. It arrests attention.

GEPETTO	That's very kind of you. Thank you very much. And I really will look after. . . .
CRICKET	Listen.

> [*In the distance we hear* PINOCCHIO *laughing and calling to someone to run faster. He enters through audience pursued by a fat and rather harrassed* POLICEMAN.]
>
> NOTE H.

POLICEMAN	Wait till I catch you, young feller me lad. . . .

> [*Other dialogue between them, improvised according to length of chase.* (13)
> *Eventually they run on to stage and* PINOCCHIO *sits down and roars with laughter. The* POLICEMAN *is about to lay hands on him when* GEPETTO *intervenes.*]

GEPETTO	Stop! (14) Why are you chasing him?
POLICEMAN	Why? I'll tell you why. There was I just calmly going along on me beat, when this—this—er—when he comes round the corner like a whirlwind and knocks me for six. Not content with that, he thinks he'll have a game with me, and he's raced me half round the town. Telling me he can go faster than I can. Puff. Never heard the like.
PINOCCHIO	Well, I did, didn't I?
POLICEMAN	Did you indeed? I'll give you run, my boy.
GEPETTO	No, please. It's all very difficult, but please let me explain. There, there, please *listen*. Now! Have you looked carefully at Pinocchio? See? See, he isn't a boy at all. He's a puppet.
POLICEMAN	[*staring at* PINOCCHIO] A what——?
GEPETTO	A puppet. My puppet. I've only just finished making him.
POLICEMAN	That's no excuse for him knocking me into the gutter.
GEPETTO	Well, it is in a way. You see, a few minutes ago, he couldn't walk at all. But he tried and he tried and he tried and—suddenly—woosh—he could do it. Then, before you could say 'Policeman's truncheon', he was off and out of sight. But really it's only because he's so excited about learning how to walk and run.
POLICEMAN	Are you having me on?
GEPETTO	No, no, really I'm not.
CRICKET	It's all perfectly true, constable. I saw it all happen.
PINOCCHIO	That's right. I ran and I ran and I ran and then—boom—I banged into your fat—your tummy.
POLICEMAN	Well, it all seems a bit fishy to me. Still, I suppose it's true enough. Come to think of it, he must be a puppet, otherwise his head wouldn't be so hard. All right. Good day to you. And watch where you're going in future, eh?

PINOCCHIO	Oh yes, I will. I'm very sorry about it all.
GEPETTO	Good day, constable.

[*The* POLICEMAN *goes.*]

PINOCCHIO	Ooooh, Pop, it's wonderful running. Thank you for teaching me.
GEPETTO	That's all right, Pinocchio, but you must be careful. You can't go running into people. You might hurt somebody.
PINOCCHIO	Who's that?
GEPETTO	That's my very great friend, Cricket.
PINOCCHIO	How do you do. Can you run?
CRICKET	I never need to. I just disappear.
PINOCCHIO	Oh! Do you? Can you teach me to do that?
CRICKET	Don't think I can. No need to, anyway, if you can run.
GEPETTO	Now, my son, you've got to get ready to go to school.
PINOCCHIO	School? What's that?
GEPETTO	Well, it's hum—er, it's, hum——
CRICKET	It's a place where boys and girls go to find out all about everything in the world.
PINOCCHIO	Really? Like running and disappearing?
GEPETTO	Well, ye-es, and one or two other things as well.
PINOCCHIO	But are puppets allowed to go?
GEPETTO	Well, I don't suppose one's ever been before. But that's no reason why you shouldn't—if you'd like to. (15)
PINOCCHIO	Yes, yes, I think I would.
GEPETTO	Good. But first I must find you some clothes. Ah! Here we are. And I'm sure friend Cricket will help you get dressed.
PINOCCHIO	Why, where are you going?
GEPETTO	I'm just going along the road to get you a spelling book. You'll need one of those for school.
PINOCCHIO	Will I? A spelling book?
GEPETTO	Yes, it's very important. D'you mind, friend Cricket?
CRICKET	Not a bit. See you soon.

[GEPETTO *goes off to get a spelling book. The* CRICKET *is a bit clumsy in helping to dress* PINOCCHIO, *so the dressing up is a matter for some mirth. Dialogue can be settled at rehearsals. At last* PINOCCHIO *is all set.*] (16)

NOTES

(15) The audience might be asked what they think about all this.

(16) Again, no need for hard work trying to get laughs. The Cricket is both clumsy and mystified, and Pinocchio doesn't know the difference between a shoe and a glove. It is this that brings shared delight, rather than hysterical yells.

CRICKET   And you look very smart, too. Like it?

PINOCCHIO   Yes, I think I do. Tell me, please? What's it really like
             at school?

CRICKET   I enjoyed it. Rather what you make it, you know.

PINOCCHIO   Then I think I'm going to like it.

CRICKET   By the way, Pinocchio. . . .
             [*Before the solemn words of advice can come out,*
             GEPETTO *returns with the spelling book. He is now,
             however, without his coat.*]

GEPETTO   Here we are, Pinocchio—my, you look smart.

PINOCCHIO   Do I, Pop? Look—I've got a lovely coat on. Oh, but
             Pop, where's *your* coat?

GEPETTO   My coat? Oh, I must have left it in the shop. I took it
             off in there because it was so stuffy. Here's your
             spelling book.

PINOCCHIO   A spelling book. Oooh, I like this. But I don't know
             what it says. C-A-T. What could that be?
             [*He takes pleasure in the audience's help.*]

PINOCCHIO   M-O-U-S-E.
             [*Audience again.*]

PINOCCHIO   Oooh. Here's a big one. C-H-R-I-S-T-M-A-S.
             [*Audience again.*]

PINOCCHIO   And this one. S-C-H-O-O-L.
             [*The school bell is heard in the distance.*]

GEPETTO   That's the school bell. You'll have to hurry.

PINOCCHIO   All right. Bye-bye, Pop. Bye-bye, Cricket.

GEPETTO   Just a minute. You don't know how to get there.

PINOCCHIO   Oh, no. So I don't.

GEPETTO   Well, it's quite easy. You turn to your left along that
             road and then to your right. Quite easy. You can't
             miss it.

PINOCCHIO   Left? Right? What are they?

GEPETTO   Well, that's your left hand, and that's your right.

CRICKET   Oh, no. Other way round. *That's* left and that's right.
             [*General muddle because of their facing* PINOCCHIO.
             Eventually it is sorted out.]

GEPETTO   Yes, yes, of course. Of course, that's it.

PINOCCHIO   I've got it, thank you. First left, then first right, and
             follow the music. Bye-bye.

GEP. & CRIC. Bye-bye. Enjoy yourself.
             [GEPETTO *and* CRICKET *go into* GEPETTO's *house.*
             PINOCCHIO *starts on road to school. He walks slowly
             along. Stops.*]

PINOCCHIO   [*listening*] That's funny. The music's stopped. Listen!
             [*From the distance is heard the pom-pom, pom-pom
             of the puppet show procession returning.*]

PINOCCHIO   No, it hasn't stopped. It's coming this way. Well, that's
             wonderful. Instead of me going to school, school's
             coming to me. I think I'll wait.

(17) Perhaps Fire-Eater would invite some of the audience to help put it up.

	[The music gets louder, and soon all of FIRE-EATER's *Company return. They all walk through the audience,* PINOCCHIO *joining them, and then on to the stage area. The puppet theatre and the puppets are erected, but this time not as for a performance, but for a rehearsal.* PINOCCHIO *stands watching these operations, which are performed under the personal supervision of* MR FIRE-EATER.*]* (17)
FIRE-EATER	That's it—up with it as quickly as you can. The sooner it's up, the sooner we can rehearse. And the sooner we rehearse, the sooner you'll be able to go home. *[to* PINOCCHIO*]* Out of the way now, my lad. There's a good chap.
PINOCCHIO	Excuse me, sir, but is this—is this. . . .
FIRE-EATER	Yes, that's right, my boy. Fire-Eater's world famous puppet show. But we're not going to do a show now. Just a rehearsal of one or two bits. You can watch if you like—but please go and sit over there, out of the way.
	*[*PINOCCHIO *does so—in audience. When all is ready, including the stringing-up of the puppets,* FIRE-EATER *says:]*
FIRE-EATER	Well, I must go and see about the handbills and posters. Won't be long. While I'm doing that, you run them through that first bit, will you?
MANIPU-LATORS	Yes, sir.
	[They climb up. FIRE-EATER *exits. Once again we see part of the Harlequinade. Then suddenly* HARLEQUIN *stops. It makes no difference how hard his strings are pulled, he just stands, flopping, and staring at* PINOCCHIO *in the audience.]*
COLUMBINE	What's the matter, Harlequin?
HARLEQUIN	Look! *[pointing at* PINOCCHIO*]*
COLUMBINE	Where?
HARLEQUIN	Out there.
	*[*PANTALONE *also stops and stares.]*
PANTALONE	Gosh!
COLUMBINE	But what is it?
HARLEQUIN	I can't believe it. Look. A puppet.
COLUMBINE	A puppet?
HARLEQUIN	Yes, one of our brothers.
PANTALONE	Gosh!
COLUMBINE	So it is. I wonder who he is.
HARLEQUIN	Let's call him.
COLUMBINE	All right.
BOTH	Hello there.

PINOCCHIO	Me?
BOTH	Yes, come up here.
PINOCCHIO	What, up there with you?
HARLEQUIN	Yes, come on.
COLUMBINE	Quickly.
PINOCCHIO	But—I—I can't do that.
HARLEQUIN	Yes, you can.
COLUMBINE	It's quite all right, really.

[PINOCCHIO *approaches the three of them.*]

HARLEQUIN	We don't often see other puppets. How do you do. This is Columbine, and I'm Harlequin.
PANTALONE	Ahem. Brrrrr.
HARLEQUIN	Oh, and that's Pantalone.
PINOCCHIO	How do you do. I'm Pinocchio.
PANTALONE	Gosh!
COLUMBINE	Oh, but look! LOOK!
HARLEQUIN	What?
COLUMBINE	He—hasn't—got—any—strings.
PANTALONE	Gosh!
HARLEQUIN	So you haven't. What's happened to your strings?
PINOCCHIO	I don't have any.
COLUMBINE	None at all?
PINOCCHIO	No. My Pop taught me how to do without them.
PANTALONE	Gosh!
COLUMBINE	Isn't that wonderful? No strings. Oh, Harlequin, wouldn't it be nice if we didn't have to use them?
HARLEQUIN	Wouldn't it?
PINOCCHIO	Well, you don't *have* to, you know. It's all a matter of practice. Why don't you try?
COLUMBINE	Oh, we couldn't. Mr Fire-Eater would never let us.
PINOCCHIO	He might. Ask him.
HARLEQUIN	Well, I suppose there's no harm in asking. Shall we?
COLUMBINE	Yes. Come on. Let's.
PANTALONE	Gosh!
BOTH	[*calling*] Mr Fire-Eater. Mr Fire-Eater.
FIRE-EATER	[*off*] Eh? Eh? What's all this shouting?
HARLEQUIN	Could we see you for a moment, please, Mr Fire-Eater?
FIRE-EATER	[*coming on*] See me? I should think not indeed. Good heavens. What do you think you're doing? Why aren't you rehearsing? [*to* MANIPULATORS *on high— who have, by now, given up, and just sit listening in astonishment*] You, there. What do you think you're playing at? Eh? What d'you think I pay you for?
TICKET S.	Please, Mr Fire-Eater. They just took it into their own hands to stop, and it made no difference how much we pulled the strings. They just would not go on.
FIRE-EATER	They wouldn't, wouldn't they? Well, we'll soon see about that. Now what do you think you're doing? [*he stops them each time they try to speak*] No, don't

	speak, don't speak. Not till you're spoken to. Now you, Pantalone. You're the eldest here. You say something.
PANTALONE	Gosh!
FIRE-EATER	I'll give you gosh. Just a minute. Stand still everyone. Perfectly still. There's something wrong here. There are too many of you. Don't speak. Let me think. [*he counts on his fingers*] Harlequin—one. Columbine —two. Pantalone—three. Three! That's what it should be. Now, stand still. Let me count you. One —two—three, and [*pointing at* PINOCCHIO] four. Gracious me. Who are you? I've seen you before somewhere. Who are you? What are you doing here? Thought I told you to go away.
	[*The* CLOWN *helps—i.e.* muddles—*the counting on his drum.*]
PINOCCHIO	Please, Mr Fire-Eater, my name's Pinocchio. I came to see your wonderful—wonderful——
FIRE-EATER	Thank you. Yes, it's a very good show. Agreed.
COLUMBINE	And we called him up here because it's such a long time since we saw another puppet.
FIRE-EATER	Oh, is that all? Then why didn't you say so?
HARLEQUIN	No, Mr Fire-Eater, it's not quite all. Have you looked at Pinocchio very carefully?
FIRE-EATER	Carefully? Yes, of course I've looked at him carefully. Fire-Eater looks at everybody carefully.
HARLEQUIN	Well, just look again. [*he does so*] Notice anything unusual about him?
FIRE-EATER	Eh? Unusual?
COLUMBINE	Have another look, Mr Fire-Eater. Now look at us. And again at Pinocchio.
	[*Slowly it dawns on* FIRE-EATER.]
FIRE-EATER	Gosh! Well I never. No strings.
HARLEQUIN	But that's still not all, Mr Fire-Eater. Pinocchio says that *we* can be like him, that it's only a matter of practice. . . .
FIRE-EATER	I don't believe it. Impossible.
PINOCCHIO	It isn't you know. Really I could help.
COLUMBINE	Would you let us try, please, Mr Fire-Eater?
FIRE-EATER	Try? Of course you can try. But it's impossible, I tell you. Impossible.

NOTES

31

(18)   This is a repetition, on a much larger scale, of the problems which confronted Pinocchio and Gepetto after Pinocchio's 'birth'.

	[*Dialogue for rest of this episode should be built up during rehearsals. With* PINOCCHIO'*s demonstration, and he and* FIRE-EATER *and the* MANIPULATORS *helping to hold the puppets up—they gradually get their* balance *and slowly master the problems involved in* walking *and* running *without the aid of strings.* HARLEQUIN *and* COLUMBINE *become more and more excited, and* PANTALONE *more and more goshful—he is quite the clumsiest of the lot.*] (18)
FIRE-EATER	It's amazing. They've done it. They've done it. Music. Music for a dance.
	[*To the tune of 'Little Rock-Get-Away' the six of them do a tremendous puppet dance, eventually falling in a heap on top of one another.* FIRE-EATER *disentangles himself from the bodies, and rescues* PINOCCHIO *from underneath them all.*]
FIRE-EATER	Pinocchio, it's wonderful. Wonderful! How can I ever thank you? Now my show will be more famous than ever. Fire-Eater's Puppets—the Only Stringless Puppets in the World. Do you hear that everyone? Only stringless puppets in the world. Come along my friends. We must make new posters and handbills at once. This very night. Excuse us, Pinocchio, and come and see us any time you like. To work, my friends, to work.
	[*And to the rhythms of the big bass drum the puppet troupe go into* FIRE-EATER'*s house, with their equipment. When the big drum stops we hear* GEPETTO *calling from within his house.*]
GEPETTO	Hello there! Is that you, Pinocchio?
PINOCCHIO	Yes, it's me, Pop.
GEPETTO	Come along in then. It's time for bed.
PINOCCHIO	Coming, Pop.
	[*He goes indoors.*]
GEPETTO	Well, now, Pinocchio, have you had a good day at school?
PINOCCHIO	I didn't get to school, Pop.
GEPETTO	Didn't get to school? How was that?
PINOCCHIO	Well, I followed the music—and then it stopped—and then it started again and came towards me. So I waited and followed it back here—to Mr Fire-Eater's house.
GEPETTO	Ha, ha, ha, you funny puppet you. That wasn't the school music. The school music's the bell.
PINOCCHIO	Only the bell?
GEPETTO	Yes. The other belongs to the puppet theatre.
PINOCCHIO	Well, I like the puppet theatre. I taught them how to work without strings—just like you taught me.
GEPETTO	Did you? When?

33

PINOCCHIO	Just now. Outside here.
GEPETTO	So that's what all the noise was. I thought they were rehearsing.

[GEPETTO *starts to make* PINOCCHIO's *bed.*]

PINOCCHIO	Well, they were to start with, but after I had shown them all how to work without strings, we all danced. Mr Fire-Eater seemed very pleased about it.
GEPETTO	I should think so too. You know, Pinocchio, I made those puppets for Mr Fire-Eater. Years ago.
PINOCCHIO	Well, they're jolly good puppets, Pop, and now they're better than ever.
GEPETTO	D'you mean to say you actually taught them yourself?
PINOCCHIO	Yes, just the same way as you taught me.
GEPETTO	Well done, Pinocchio. That's a grand day's work. Oh well, school can wait until tomorrow. Now, off to bed with you.
PINOCCHIO	Bed? What's bed?
GEPETTO	[*pointing to it*] This is your bed. You lie on it and cover yourself with the blankets—and then you go fast to sleep. Aren't you tired?
PINOCCHIO	Well, I feel a bit wobbly about the knees. Is that being tired?
GEPETTO	It most certainly is. Go on—in you jump. Have a good sleep and then you'll be ready for school tomorrow.

[PINOCCHIO *gets into bed with all his clothes on.*]

GEPETTO	Hey, wait a minute. Take your clothes off first.

[*By now* PINOCCHIO *is very wobbly. He just manages to undress, then falls into bed and is asleep instantly.*]

NOTES

GEPETTO He's asleep already. [*coming to audience*] Just fancy that—my Pinocchio teaching all those clever puppets. Isn't it wonderful? [*suddenly remembering*] Oh dear. Deary me—he hasn't washed, he hasn't cleaned his teeth and he hasn't said his prayers. Never mind he can do them in the morning. [*yawns*] Oohh—I'm a bit sleepy too. Think I'll turn in now. It's been an exciting day, what with wishes coming true and—and—no. Ohhh. It's no good. I can't keep awake any longer. [*to audience*] Why don't you go to sleep too? I expect you're tired. Go on. All of you. I'll wake you in the morning. And if I don't the cock will—he crows incredibly loudly round these parts. Go on then. Off to sleep with you. Goodnight.

[*He goes back into his house—then puts his head either through the door, or out of the window.*]

By the way, thank you for helping me wish like that. It did work, didn't it? Oh, sorry. Were you nearly asleep? All right, I won't talk any more. Goodnight.

[*He puts the light out. Darkness. Silence.*] (19)

END OF ACT I

NOTES

(19) If they sleep in view of the audience (and they should) and if there is no curtain (and there shouldn't be) then they must stay asleep throughout the interval. People will come to see if they are—if they genuinely are they will be left in peace. If woken, they could ask to be left in peace.

(Sorry about their cup of tea—they must have it in the second interval instead.)

ACT II

During the interval there should be displayed notices saying, PLEASE GO TO SLEEP AGAIN WHEN YOU RETURN TO YOUR SEATS, or some such.

(It is essential that these notices be displayed only during this interval—they will be confusing if seen before the play or during the second interval.) A note to the same effect should be inserted in the programme. When all are re-seated, the theatre should be blacked out. Everyone sleeps. There is complete silence. (20)

Dawn breaks. A cock crows twice. Light fades up on the stage area (the East). GEPETTO *wakes—stretches and scratches himself. He comes out of his house and moves sleepily towards the audience.*

GEPETTO   [*in a polite early morning whisper*] Good morning. Are you awake? Sorry to disturb you all. But you did ask me to wake you, didn't you? You know—I think it's going to be rather a nice day. Oh! Pinocchio! He ought to be getting up too. [*moving to house*] Wake up, Pinocchio. Wake up. Come on old son—shake a leg.

PINOCCHIO   [*yawning*] Ahhhh. Who is it?

GEPETTO   It's me—Pop. Come on—it's time to wake up and go to school.

PINOCCHIO   Ooh yes. School. Of course. I must hurry.
           [PINOCCHIO *is dressing during next section of dialogue.*]

GEPETTO   [*confidentially*] Pinocchio—there's something we forgot last night.

PINOCCHIO   Was there? What was that, Pop?

GEPETTO   Face, hands, teeth.

PINOCCHIO   Face, hands, teeth! Face, hands, teeth? What about them?

GEPETTO   We didn't wash them.

PINOCCHIO   No, we didn't. Should we have done?

GEPETTO   Oh yes. Always at night, and again in the morning.

PINOCCHIO   Why?

GEPETTO   Why? Well, er—because it's best to have clean hands and face for meals, and very nice to have shining white teeth.

PINOCCHIO   Oh. Then we'd better do them now, hadn't we?

GEPETTO   Yes, I think so.

PINOCCHIO   [*looking at audience*] All of us?
           NOTE J.

GEPETTO   Ooh, yes. Everybody, that is, who's got hands and faces and teeth.

PINOCCHIO   [*to audience*] Oh, well, we'd better get on with it, hadn't we?

[The remainder of this sequence should be built up in rehearsals. PINOCCHIO *will lead the whole audience in washing and drying, cleaning their teeth, brushing their hair, cleaning shoes, etc. (i.e. activities that can be done sitting down). After this there is breakfast to cook—all can again join in this.]* (21) *When* GEPETTO *and* PINOCCHIO *are both ready for work:]*

NOTES

J   From this point onwards, Pinocchio is taking over the main responsibility for participation. This is essential because:

    (a) Gepetto is about to disappear till the middle of Act III.

    (b) Pinocchio is going to be in great need of the audience's help shortly.

(20) It doesn't matter if there aren't any lights.

(21) No comic business should be worked out for this scene or else the audience is tacitly invited to *watch*—not to *do*. All that is required is for Pinocchio and Gepetto to genuinely and sincerely get on with their ablutions and cooking, etc., and perhaps lend their soap or toothpaste and so on. It is essential that no props are used for this sequence—otherwise the audience will not join in so readily. Pinocchio's aim should be to get everyone participating and then to remain absorbed in his own ablutions, etc. In this way the audience will 'do' without necessarily copying Pinocchio move for move. The same sincerity applied to the end of Act I and the opening of this Act should remain—i.e. there should be no comic pantomime crosstalk about 'Don't forget behind your ears lady', etc. Ears can legitimately come into it, but must remain an integral part of the scene. Accuracy in mime is essential for Gepetto and Pinocchio, but they should not worry the youngsters about this

37

GEPETTO	Well, it's time we were both off, Pinocchio. I must go and see Antonio about some new logs, and I must buy some paint, and, oh dear, oh dear, so many things to buy and no money to buy them with. Never mind. One day, maybe, when I've made lots of puppets like you—then perhaps we shall have more money.
PINOCCHIO	I hope so, Pop.
GEPETTO	There, but don't you worry about that, Pinocchio. Now, you know your way to school *this* time, don't you?
PINOCCHIO	Oh yes—first left [*raising right hand*] and then first right [*raising left hand*].
GEPETTO	Well, that's nearly right. It is first left and then first right—but *that's* your left hand, and that's your right. Don't forget, will you? Well, bye-bye. Have a good day at school.
PINOCCHIO	Bye-bye, Pop.
	[GEPETTO *exits.* PINOCCHIO *stands waving goodbye —then starts to move towards audience.*]
PINOCCHIO	[*muttering*] Left hand, right hand, first left, first right. . . . [*There comes a large welcoming yawning sound from* FIRE-EATER's *house. The door opens and* FIRE-EATER *comes out.* PINOCCHIO *stands watching him do his daily dozen—getting a bit tangled up in his beard in the process.*]
PINOCCHIO	Good morning, Mr Fire-Eater.
FIRE-EATER	Eh? Ah, good morning, Pinocchio. A very good morning, my friend. Ahha. I have something to show you. Wait one moment, please—I'll fetch it. [*He goes back into his house and returns with one of his new posters announcing* 'the only stringless puppets in the world.']
FIRE-EATER	There, my friend. That is what you have done for me. It's wonderful. How can I ever thank you?
PINOCCHIO	Don't thank me, Mr Fire-Eater. It's not me that did it. It's my Pop.
FIRE-EATER	Your Pop must be a very clever man, Pinocchio.
PINOCCHIO	He's the cleverest man in the whole world.
FIRE-EATER	You thank him for me, won't you?
PINOCCHIO	Yes, I will.
FIRE-EATER	Is he a rich man?
PINOCCHIO	No, I think he's very, very poor.
FIRE-EATER	Oh, and what makes you think that?
PINOCCHIO	Well, he went out to buy me this spelling book yesterday, and when he came back he hadn't got a coat on.
FIRE-EATER	And you think he sold it to buy the spelling book—eh?
PINOCCHIO	I'm sure he did. And only a minute ago he was telling

	me that he hadn't enough money to buy the logs and paints and things that he needs.
FIRE-EATER	Logs and paints? What does he need them for?
PINOCCHIO	To make puppets.
FIRE-EATER	Oh, he makes puppets, does he?
PINOCCHIO	Of course he does. He made me.
FIRE-EATER	[*the light dawning*] Just a minute, Pinocchio. You don't mean to tell me that your Pop is my friend, Mr Gepetto?
PINOCCHIO	Of course he is.
FIRE-EATER	Ah, and I didn't know. I had no idea at all. This is very fine news. I've bought many of my finest puppets from your father.
PINOCCHIO	I know. He was telling me last night.
FIRE-EATER	But I had no idea he was so poor. And he's never told me. Here—you must give him these few gold pieces. They will buy him a new coat and some paint and some logs. And when he comes home I'll ask him to make me some more of his wonderful puppets.
PINOCCHIO	That's very nice of you, Mr Fire-Eater. But I don't think I ought to take your money.
FIRE-EATER	Oh yes, you ought. I happen to be a very rich man— and after what you and your Pop have done for us all, I shall be richer still. Go on—put it in your pocket, and off you go to school. You'll be very late.
PINOCCHIO	Thank you very much, Mr Fire-Eater. See you this evening.
FIRE-EATER	Come and see me any time you like, my friend. Bye-bye.
	[FIRE-EATER *waves from the door of his house and goes inside.* PINOCCHIO *stands for a moment talking to the audience.*]
PINOCCHIO	[*counting the gold pieces*] One, two, three, four, five. (22) Gosh. Five gold pieces. Wasn't that nice of him? Pop will be pleased. Oh, listen. (23)
	[COLUMBINE's *head appears round the arch behind* PINOCCHIO.]
COLUMBINE	Pssst.
	[PINOCCHIO *looks up. Quickly* HARLEQUIN's *head appears from opposite arch.*]
HARLEQUIN	Pssst.

NOTES

(22) Pinocchio could get co-operation with the counting.
(23) Such words as 'listen' help to cool any excitement that might arise from participation in such things as the counting.

PINOCCHIO	What was that?
	[*The audience may say, 'Behind you', or some such. The matter is settled for* PANTALONE's *head appears lower down with——*]
PANTALONE	Gosh!
	[PINOCCHIO *turns and sees them.*]
PINOCCHIO	Oh, hello.
	[*Quietly they come down to him and surround him, talking as they come.*]
HARLEQUIN	We wanted to see you——
COLUMBINE	If you can spare the time——
HARLEQUIN	It's very important——
COLUMBINE	And terribly exciting.
HARLEQUIN	We didn't sleep a wink last night——
COLUMBINE	And couldn't even eat our breakfast——
PANTALONE	Gosh!
	[*They both turn on him.*]
BOTH	Except Pantalone. He's always eating or sleeping.
PINOCCHIO	But what was it you wanted to see me for?
COLUMBINE	Oh, you'll never guess.
HARLEQUIN	It's very secret.
COLUMBINE	Mr Fire-Eater doesn't know——
HARLEQUIN	Nor Candlewick——
COLUMBINE	Nor anyone——
PANTALONE	Gosh!
BOTH	Except Pantalone.
PINOCCHIO	But what is it?
BOTH	*We've written a song.*
PINOCCHIO	A song?
COLUMBINE	Yes. A lovely song.
HARLEQUIN	Such a funny song.
COLUMBINE	We made it all up——
HARLEQUIN	In bed last night.
PINOCCHIO	What's it called?
COLUMBINE	Puppetitus.
PINOCCHIO	What?
COLUMBINE	Puppetitus.
HARLEQUIN	The song of the stringless puppets.
PINOCCHIO	How wonderful. Can I hear it?
BOTH	Yes, yes, yes. Of course you can.
PANTALONE	Gosh!
COLUMBINE	Be quiet, Pantalone.
HARLEQUIN	Sit down here, Pinocchio.
	[*They bustle* PINOCCHIO *to his seat, and prepare to sing their song. IDEA—No music accompaniment. The words are made up by the actors.* COLUMBINE *has bells,*

	HARLEQUIN *has pins in tins,* PANTALONE *has a drum. Part of the rhythm is built by* PANTALONE'S *'Gosh'. The beat is so simple that the audience could easily join in. The sequence might end with a dance. Then the school bell is heard again.* PINOCCHIO *suddenly remembers school, hastily says farewell and thanks to the puppets, who bustle back into* MR FIRE-EATER'S *house.*]
PINOCCHIO	I must hurry.
	[*He hurries through the auditorium, round the top and down towards the stage again. As he approaches the stage,* FOX *and* CAT *skirt the front of it and bar* PINOCCHIO'S *path. They are a couple of plausible rogues—they bow to* PINOCCHIO *with a flourish.*]
FOX & CAT	A jolly good day to you, Pinocchio.
PINOCCHIO	Thank you. And a good day to you. [*he stops as he passes them*] But—how do you know my name?
CAT	We happen to be very dear friends of Mr Gepetto. He's Fox and I'm Cat.
PINOCCHIO	How d'you do. It's strange you know, but I don't remember my Pop ever mentioning you two. I suppose that's because he's been very busy.
	[FOX *and* CAT *exchange looks and a look with the audience.*]
	NOTE K.
CAT	[*in a whisper*] A simpleton, I think.
FOX	[*in a whisper*] We shall have no trouble with him.
PINOCCHIO	Anyway, I'll tell Pop I met you. That's the second piece of exciting news today.
FOX	The second?
CAT	And what was the first?
PINOCCHIO	Look, there's the first.
	[*He opens his hand and* FOX *and* CAT *peer at the gold.*]

NOTES

K   Fox and Cat will get little enough sympathy from the audience, but should build a bond all the same. Also at this point they should quickly see where in their chases they should not stop or perhaps even go, because of young or over-sensitive children. Much information on these points will have been gleaned by other members of the cast, who should pass on their news very carefully to Fox and Cat.

FOX	Well, well, well—how lucky you are, Pinocchio.
CAT	Most fortunate.
PINOCCHIO	Mr Fire-Eater gave them to me.
FOX	How very nice of him.
CAT	Most, most generous.
FOX	Five *hundred* pieces of gold.
CAT	Five *thousand* pieces of gold.
PINOCCHIO	No, no. Just plain five.
FOX	Ah, but those five could become five hundred.
CAT	Or even five thousand.
PINOCCHIO	How?
FOX	Ahhhhhh.
CAT	Ahhhhhh.
PINOCCHIO	Oh!
FOX	Of course, we could do it for you.
CAT	It wouldn't take long.
FOX	All you'd have to do would be to give us the gold pieces.
CAT	And in ten minutes we'd be back with sacks full of it.

[*There is suddenly the sound of a* FROG *croaking (the Fairy again) from off.*]

FROG	Don't listen to them, Pinocchio. Don't listen.
FOX	What was that?
PINOCCHIO	I've no idea.
CAT	Sounded like a frog to me.
FROG	Don't take any notice of them, Pinocchio. Hang on to your gold.
FOX & CAT	Ahhhhhh.

[*They move stealthily away from* PINOCCHIO, *who is now looking round for the* FROG.]

FOX	We shall have to try other methods, Mr Cat.
CAT	Indeed we shall, Mr Fox.
FOX	Come quickly.

[*They exit stealthily.*]

PINOCCHIO	[*still searching*] Where are you Frog?
FROG	Over here, Pinocchio. Behind these trees.
PINOCCHIO	Where?

[*With one bound the* FROG *lands just by* PINOCCHIO.]

PINOCCHIO	Oh, hello!
FROG	I mustn't stay here long in case they see me.
PINOCCHIO	In case who sees you?
FROG	The robbers and highwaymen.
PINOCCHIO	Robbers and highwaymen? Who are they?
FROG	People who try to steal your money. Be very careful, Pinocchio. Look after your gold until you can give it to Mr Gepetto. Look out—someone's coming now. I will help you if I can.

[*And again with one bound the* FROG *returns to its hiding place.*]

PINOCCHIO	I wonder who's coming. I didn't hear anyone. Perhaps it's my friends Fox and Cat. I wonder where they went to.

> [*He moves along to look up one of the stage area streets. At that moment Two Highwaymen (*FOX *and* CAT *disguised in cloaks and masks and three-cornered hats) appear.*]

FOX	Stay where you are.
CAT	Quite still, please.
PINOCCHIO	Why?
FOX	No questions please.
CAT	Hand over your money.
FOX	Quickly.
PINOCCHIO	But I haven't got any.
FOX	Oh yes, you have.
CAT	Give it to us.
PINOCCHIO	But I've only got five pieces of gold and they aren't really mine to give. They belong to my Pop.
FOX	We don't care who they belong to.
CAT	Hand them over quickly.
PINOCCHIO	No, I won't.
FOX	We'll give you up till ten——
CAT	And then——
FOX & CAT	One—two——

> [*With each number they take one step—manoeuvring themselves until they are on either side of* PINOCCHIO, *closing in for a final pounce.*]

FOX & CAT	Three—four——
FROG	[*off*] Wait till nine, Pinocchio. Then run.
FOX & CAT	Five—six—seven—eight—nine——
FROG	[*off*] Run, Pinocchio. Run.

> [PINOCCHIO *suddenly dashes forward. At the same time* FOX *and* CAT *spring—and land on top of one another, half fighting, thinking they have got* PINOCCHIO. *Dialogue is improvised.*]
> *In the meantime,* PINOCCHIO *flees up one of the auditorium gangways, and gets himself hidden.*
> NOTE L.

NOTES

L   By this time Pinocchio will *know* those sections of the audience where he will find protection. Here he can hide, and ask that Fox and Cat be mis-directed. On no account should he lose his absorption as Pinocchio, for it is Pinocchio only that people will want to help.

M   This is not the *major* chase of the act so the actors involved need to keep something in reserve and also make sure the audience has something in reserve.

For this and the other chases, it is very essential there be some pre-training so that the three actors do not fall over or knock into any members of the audience who may run into gangways.

Care must be taken to avoid going near any people in the audience who may be frightened by the chase—fright can often arise from an actor suddenly stopping and peering too closely into the faces of tiny children.

N   It may well happen on occasions that the audience is so concerned with Pinocchio's welfare that they refuse to allow him to talk to Fox and Cat but insist instead that he goes to school. If they do this with some vigour, then there is no point in trying to stick to the next few pages of script. Better by far to let Pinocchio accept the advice and run away with Fox and Cat in pursuit. Pinocchio could then call for the Policeman and Fox and Cat hide when he appears—thence into the detective scene (*see page* 48). Of course the lines about having been robbed would have to be changed, but no doubt Fox and Cat are notorious enough for the police to want to capture them anyway. Similarly, if such a course was taken, a few of the lines between Pinocchio and the Policeman in the scene after the capture of Fox and Cat (*see page* 51) would need to be changed.

	FOX *and* CAT *realise their mistake and set off to look for* PINOCCHIO—*asking various people in the audience where he has gone. Either the audience don't know or else they misdirect them.* (FOX *can give a lead to the audience, and, if by any chance the right directions are given, then the chase can be extended.*) *Eventually they find him and a chase ensues.*

NOTE M.

They catch PINOCCHIO *and take him to the stage area.*]

FOX You hold him still, while I search his pockets.

[PINOCCHIO *struggles—and then, just as it seems that* FOX *and* CAT *are going to overpower him, there is a tremendous croaking noise. The* FROG *jumps in and runs circles round* FOX *and* CAT, *eventually scaring, pushing, or chasing them off, with* PINOCCHIO's *help.*]

FROG Phew. That was close.

PINOCCHIO Thank you very much, Frog.

FROG That's all right. Now perhaps you can see what I mean about being careful.

PINOCCHIO I will be, don't worry. Gosh, I'm going to be late for school.

FROG Yes, you are.

PINOCCHIO Oh, but I'm so puffed. I'll sit down for one minute, just to get my breath back, and then I'll run all the way to school. You know, Frog, none of this would have happened if Mr Fox and Mr Cat hadn't disappeared. I wonder where they went.

FROG You mean to say you don't know who the highwaymen were?

FOX & CAT [*off*] Pinocchio. Pinocchio.

FROG Oh. Be careful, Pinocchio. I'll hide again.

[FROG *leaps away into hiding as* FOX *and* CAT (*once more themselves*) *re-appear very hot and tired.*]

NOTE N.

PINOCCHIO Hello. You two look a bit puffed. Have you been running?

FOX Yes, we have—all the way——

CAT And we have—some very good news for you, Pinocchio.

PINOCCHIO What good news?

FOX Sit you down——

CAT And we'll tell you all about it.

PINOCCHIO [*as they sit*] I mustn't stay long. I'm very late for school as it is.

FOX We won't keep you five minutes.

CAT Not even four minutes.

PINOCCHIO Well?

FOX	You remember what we said about making your five gold pieces into five hundred?
CAT	Or even five thousand.
PINOCCHIO	Yes, I remember.
FOX	Well, we've just been to see our very good friend who owns the Field of Miracles——
CAT	And he says he'll be delighted to help you——
FOX	Now. At once.
CAT	This very moment.
PINOCCHIO	The Field of Miracles? What's that?
FOX	You don't know the Field of Miracles?
PINOCCHIO	No.
FOX	Ohh, but it's an amazing place——
CAT	Simply magnificent.
FOX	All you have to do is to bury your five gold pieces——
CAT	Spray the ground with water——
FOX	Sprinkle a little salt——
CAT	Say the magic mumbo jumbo——
FOX	And in less than no time each piece of gold will grow into a golden bush——
CAT	Laden with fruit—golden fruit——
FOX	And then you'll have all the money you and your Pop need.
	[*A moment's silence.*]
PINOCCHIO	Gosh. That would help him, wouldn't it?
FROG	Don't listen, Pinocchio.
	[*But* PINOCCHIO *is too carried away by the prospect of helping* GEPETTO.]
PINOCCHIO	Would it take long? You see, while I'd do anything to help my Pop, all the same I am rather late for school.
FOX	It won't take three minutes——
CAT	One to get there——
FOX	One to bury the five gold pieces——
CAT	And less than one while they grow——
PINOCCHIO	Well, if it's that quick—I'd be silly not to go, wouldn't I?
FROG	Don't go with them, Pinocchio.
	[*But these words are lost to* PINOCCHIO *in the triumphant shouts of 'The Field of Miracles—to make a Fortune', which come from* FOX *and* CAT. *On either side of* PINOCCHIO, *they set off on their journey. The* FROG *follows them at a discreet distance, hiding if they seem to look round at all. They return to the stage area.* FROG *hides behind some different bushes.*]
FOX	Here we are.
CAT	The Field of Miracles.
PINOCCHIO	Oh, it's rather an ordinary looking field, isn't it?

46

FOX	It has to be. If it didn't look ordinary—everyone would know about it——
CAT	And then everyone would know our secret.
PINOCCHIO	Yes. I suppose they would.
FOX	Now, my friend. Just scratch away a little of this earth. [PINOCCHIO *does so.*]
CAT	And put in the five gold pieces. [PINOCCHIO *does so.* FOX *produces a packet of salt.*]
FOX	Sprinkle on some of this salt. [PINOCCHIO *does so.* CAT *produces watering can.*]
CAT	And some of this water. [PINOCCHIO *sprinkles the water.*]
FOX	And now turn round five times slowly, with your eyes tight shut——
CAT	Saying, 'Mumbo jumbo, Mumbo jumbo', all the time you're turning. [*With his eyes shut tight,* PINOCCHIO *starts turning round and round, muttering 'Mumbo jumbo' as he turns.* *And stealthily* FOX *and* CAT *dig up his five gold pieces and bolt with them.*]
FROG	[*jumping from hiding—but too late*] Look out, Pinocchio, they've stolen your gold.
PINOCCHIO	[*stopping his 'mumbo jumbo'*] Oh, hello, Frog, you still here?
FROG	Don't just stand there, Pinocchio. Don't you understand they've taken your gold?
PINOCCHIO	Who has?
FROG	Fox and Cat. They were the two robbers who tried to steal the gold just now.
PINOCCHIO	Were they?
FROG	Of course they were. I tried to warn you, but you didn't take any notice of me.
PINOCCHIO	Oh dear, oh dear—what am I going to do now? Shall we chase after them?
FROG	No, that wouldn't do any good now. They'll be miles away. In any case I could have stopped them if I wanted to—but I could only have chased them away, and I think it's time they were taught a proper lesson.
PINOCCHIO	Yes, but how?
FROG	You run as fast as you can, Pinocchio, to the Police Station—tell the police what's happened, and when they catch them they'll find the gold on them and then lock them up.
PINOCCHIO	All right. What about you?
FROG	Don't worry about me—I'll help in some way. Go on— as fast as you can.

	[*From this point up to the capture of* FOX *and* CAT *everything is more or less at top speed—so the dialogue given here is largely an indication, but it may be necessary to improvise a lot of it.*
	The FROG *exits down one of the stage area openings, and* PINOCCHIO *dashes through audience. He runs up one of the gangways, across the back and down towards the stage. As he nears it he starts calling.*]
PINOCCHIO	Police. Police. Quickly. Police.
	[*The* POLICEMAN (*the same one* PINOCCHIO *knocked down earlier*) *appears—and* PINOCCHIO *runs full pelt into him, knocking him down again.*]
POLICEMAN	[*quickly recovering*] So it's you again—I thought I told you to be more careful.
PINOCCHIO	Sorry, constable, I didn't meant to bang into you. You must help me. I've been robbed.
POLICEMAN	Robbed?
PINOCCHIO	Yes.
POLICEMAN	What of?
PINOCCHIO	Five pieces of gold.
POLICEMAN	Have you indeed? [*he fishes out a book of instructions while talking*] Robbery. Now, there's a job for the detectives. [*looks in book*] Detectives. Page five. Page five. Ah, here we are. Detectives. Three short blasts and one long one.
	[*He takes out his whistle and gives three short blasts and one long one.*
	Immediately there is a scuffling and a barking and from behind them appear two DETECTIVES—*very posh and identically dressed (rather like Sherlock Holmes) with identical enormous spy-glasses, and, on the end of identical chains—one identical, docile* BLOODHOUND *each. The* DETECTIVES *go straight to the constable.*]
DETECTIVES	[*speaking together*] You blew, constable?
POLICEMAN	Yes. This lad's been robbed.
DETECTIVES	Has he? Who by?
PINOCCHIO	Fox and Cat.
DETECTIVES	[*looking at one another*] Ah. Fox and Cat.
	[*They turn to their respective bloodhounds and bark (literally) a few crisp instructions. The dogs look at one another, and then immediately start sniffing the ground. In no time they are all in hot pursuit of* FOX *and* CAT. *They search and search and search—and eventually arrive back where they started—having found nothing. But before they can say a thing, a large* BIRD (*the Fairy again*) *swoops down to them.*]
BIRD	Quickly—this way. I spotted them while I was flying over the woods. Quickly—I'll lead.

[*And with the* BIRD *leading the way they once more set off after* FOX *and* CAT. *This time they are caught and are marched ceremoniously off to court by the* POLICEMAN.]

NOTE P.

JUDGE	Silence in the Court. Silence. [*all silent*] I'm the Judge.
POLICEMAN	I'm a policeman.
JUDGE	I know that, silly. Where are the prisoners?
POLICEMAN	Here they are, yer honour.
	[*Bloodhounds drag forward* FOX *and* CAT.]
JUDGE	What's the trouble?
POLICEMAN	They stole his money.

NOTES

P   This is the major chase and should, within limits of sensitivity about young or worried members of the audience, allow the excitement that has been mounting in this act to reach its natural climax.

D

JUDGE	Who's money?
PINOCCHIO	Mine, your honour.
JUDGE	How much money?
PINOCCHIO	Five gold pieces.
JUDGE	Gosh! (*No! It couldn't be* PANTALONE—*could it? Why not?*)
FOX & CAT	We didn't steal it.
JUDGE	Silence. Now—who caught the prisoners?
DETECTIVES	[*bowing*] We did, your honour.
POLICEMAN	No—I did, yer honour.
DOGS	[*indignantly*] Wow—wow wow, wow wow-wow.
	(No—we did, yer hon-our.)
	[*A terrific argument starts between* DETECTIVES, *the* POLICEMAN *and the* BLOODHOUNDS, *finally quelled by*—]
JUDGE	SILENCE. [*calm returns. To* FOX *and* CAT] What have you two to say?
FOX	*I* didn't steal it.
CAT	*I* didn't steal it.
OTHERS	Yes, you did.
FOX & CAT	Prove it.
JUDGE	That's right—prove it. We can't put them in prison unless someone saw them steal it. Did anyone see?
	[DETECTIVES, BLOODHOUNDS, POLICEMAN *and* PINOCCHIO *all turn to audience.*]
ALL	[*together*] Did you see them steal the money?
	[*Depending on reaction repeat*—]
	Did you?
	[*And if answer is 'yes'*—]
JUDGE	That's good enough for me. Take them away.
	[JUDGE *and* POLICEMAN *march* FOX *and* CAT *off.* PINOCCHIO *is left with* DETECTIVES *and* BLOODHOUNDS.]
PINOCCHIO	Thank you very much. It was very nice of you to help.
DETECTIVES	Not at all. Pleasure.
	[*The two* DETECTIVES *shake hands with* PINOCCHIO. *The two* DOGS *shake hands with* PINOCCHIO. *The* DETECTIVES *shake hands with each other. The* DOGS *solemnly shake paws—and then, as if nothing in the world had happened, the* DETECTIVES *with their* DOGS *and their spy-glasses return from whence they came.* PINOCCHIO *sits down.*]
	NOTE Q.

NOTES

Q Pinocchio sits down and says '*Phew*'—from him, by his actions and feelings, the calm should return in part to the audience. This will depend to an extent on how much the climax was allowed to come. *But haste should stop here* so that everyone can relax a bit.

PINOCCHIO	Phew! What a day. What an exciting day. Well, so much for Fox and Cat. It's their own silly faults—if they only did a day's work to earn some money then they wouldn't have to steal—and if they didn't steal they wouldn't land up in prison.
POLICEMAN	[off] Pinocchio.
PINOCCHIO	I'm here.
	[Enter POLICEMAN.]
POLICEMAN	Here you are, my lad. Here are your five gold pieces back again—fortunately they didn't have time to hide them let alone spend them.
PINOCCHIO	Thank you very much, constable. That's very kind of you.
POLICEMAN	Not at all. That's what we're here for. Take good care of them now, won't you?
	[From the distance we hear again the school bell.]
PINOCCHIO	I certainly will, constable. Gosh, isn't that the school bell.
POLICEMAN	Yes.
PINOCCHIO	I must hurry. Or I shall be terribly late.
	[The POLICEMAN bursts into laughter.]
PINOCCHIO	There's nothing to laugh about. I was so late yesterday, that I never got there at all—and——
POLICEMAN	Well, the same thing's happened today. Ha. Ha. Ha.
PINOCCHIO	The same thing? Again? D'you mean. . . ?
POLICEMAN	Yes—that's the bell for ending school, not going to it.
PINOCCHIO	Well, I'll be blowed. So I've missed it again. Oh dear, oh dear, what will Pop think?
POLICEMAN	Don't you worry, Pinocchio. You may not have got to school, but you've helped to catch two very dangerous robbers—and that's a good day's work. Ha. Ha. Ha.
	[And still laughing—an infectious laugh which PINOCCHIO enjoys and joins in—the POLICEMAN leaves to return to his duties. PINOCCHIO continues laughing to himself. He stops as he hears another noise—that of 'charmingly eerie music'. The sound gets nearer, and suddenly with a great fluttering of wings, the BIRD returns, breathless and urgent.]
BIRD	Quickly, Pinocchio—come with me. Your Pop's got lost somewhere and we must go and look for him.
PINOCCHIO	Lost? Where?
BIRD	Oh, don't worry. Nothing's happened to him—but he went along to school this morning to see your teacher, and when he discovered you weren't there he set off in search of you. He searched and searched and searched—and couldn't find you anywhere. So then he got into a small boat and went out to sea

51

	in case you were having adventures in some other land. And now—well, I've lost track of him.
PINOCCHIO	Oh dear. What can we do?
BIRD	Go and look for him, of course. We'll ask all the birds and the fish if they've seen him—and if they haven't we'll ask them to keep a very special look out and let us know if they find him. Now keep very near to me, Pinocchio, and then you'll be able to fly.
PINOCCHIO	Fly?
BIRD	Yes. Like me.
PINOCCHIO	But how? How can I?
BIRD	Magic. Magic that works as long as you keep very close to me. Now—try it. Go on, try.
	[*On the stage area*, PINOCCHIO, *keeping very close to the* BIRD, *flaps his arms and gradually finds that he can fly. Away they both go—through the audience, asking the birds and the fish if they have seen* MR GEPETTO. *If they have, then the two go in that direction; if they haven't, then the two ask them to keep a very special look out. Eventually they come back to the stage area.*]
	NOTE R.
PINOCCHIO	[*to audience*] Well—no luck so far. We'd better go and look somewhere else. Will you keep on looking please? A really good look. And we'll come back soon to see if you've found anything. Thank you very much. Come on, Bird. Off we go. . . .
	[*Bird music. They fly round and away—and the music fades them out of sight.*]

END OF ACT II

NOTES

R   Again Pinocchio and the Bird remain absorbed and urgent in their enquiries—it would be wiser to ask groups of people rather than individuals.

It could also be possible to change the ending given here and the Fairy could 'work her magic' over the whole audience so they too become birds and fly away to seek Gepetto. This would depend on the layout of gangways and the accessibility of exits—and if Pinocchio and the Fairy intend doing this, they should *keep moving* and collecting more birds as they move. If they stop and invite hundreds out to a stationary mob position, there will be a sudden mob surge when they eventually move and some people might get trampled. But with good wide exits and gangways it should be possible to have nearly the whole audience fly away to the second interval. This could be controlled by the music.

Act III

When the audience are back in their seats, both PINOCCHIO *and the* BIRD *repeat their journey round the audience asking if anyone has seen* GEPETTO. *Every clue is followed up—but if he has been seen somewhere, by the time the* BIRD *and* PINOCCHIO *reach that place, he has gone again. Eventually they both settle on the stage area.*

PINOCCHIO   Oh dear, oh dear, oh dear. All night we've searched, and we've asked the birds and the animals and the fish and the insects—and none of them has the slightest idea where my Pop is.

BIRD   Don't you worry, Pinocchio. We'll find him.

PINOCCHIO   But how?

BIRD   I've just had an idea. Now you get ready for school and I'll go and have another look—and before tonight I'm sure we'll find him. As soon as I do I'll come and let you know. So goodbye for now, Pinocchio. Goodbye. . . .
[*She flies away.*]

PINOCCHIO   Goodbye, Bird. Come back soon. [*to audience*] I wonder where she's gone to look now. I thought we'd searched everywhere possible. Never mind. I'm sure she'll find him, aren't you?
[*The school bell is heard in the distance.*]
Listen. There's the school bell. Oh, I do hope I get there today. Funny you know—I've been flying all night but I don't feel a bit tired. Perhaps that's because of the magic wings. Well, I can't fly now, but I can run. . . .
[*He starts to run but has hardly moved when there is the sound of a 'tin trumpet fanfare' and swooping down on him comes an imaginary coach with a* COACHMAN *lashing his imaginary horses. (This comes through the audience.) Inside the coach is* CANDLEWICK—FIRE-EATER'S *son. As the coach draws nearer to* PINOCCHIO :] (24)

CANDLEWICK   [*to coachman*] Pull up, Coachman. Here's someone else.

COACHMAN   Woa, there. Woa. . . . [*the coach stops*]

CANDLEWICK   Hello. Who are you?

PINOCCHIO   Pinocchio.

CANDLEWICK   I'm Candlewick. Jump in.

PINOCCHIO   Where are you going? School?

CANDLEWICK   School? Not likely. We've just come from school.

PINOCCHIO   Then I won't get in, thank you. I'm on my way there now.

CANDLEWICK   But we're going somewhere much better than school.

NOTES

(24)   The coach and horses are mimed.

PINOCCHIO	Where's that?
CANDLEWICK	The Land of the Boobies.
COACHMAN	It's not very far from here, young sir. Just hop in, and we'll be there in no time. It's very nice, you know. No work—nothing but play and eating and enjoying yourselves. And you needn't stay very long—just a few hours, and when you're fed up—if you ever are fed up—then I'll bring you back again.
CANDLEWICK	Aw, come on, Pinocchio—don't often get a chance like this.
PINOCCHIO	Oh, all right. But not for long. [*he gets in coach*]
COACHMAN	As you will, young sir. Gee up there. Get on with yer. [*The coach gallops away, round the audience, and on to the stage area again.*]
COACHMAN	There y'are, me beauties. Off you go then, and have a look round. I'll not be far off, I promise yer. [*He laughs rather an ugly laugh while watching* PINOCCHIO *and* CANDLEWICK, *who come on to the stage area a bit more.*]
PINOCCHIO	You know—I begin to feel a bit odd, Candlewick.
CANDLEWICK	Do you? What sort of odd?
PINOCCHIO	Well, like as if I can't keep upright—no—I can't—look, I want to bend over.
CANDLEWICK	So do I. Isn't it strange? [*And so their dialogue can be built up during rehearsal while they slowly become donkeys. They are more amused than frightened by it and gallop around the place quite gleefully. (25) Suddenly the* COACHMAN *comes from his hiding place.*]
COACHMAN	Ah, me little beauties, this has worked quicker than usual. It seldom takes less than an hour or so, and sometimes it takes a month.
PINOCCHIO	What does?
COACHMAN	Why, turning into donkeys does.
CANDLEWICK	D'you mean to say there aren't all those wonderful things you told us about in the Land of the Boobies?
COACHMAN	[*bursting with laughter*] Why, bless 'ee, no. That's just a delicious story to get 'ee here. Cos that's my trade, see. Selling donkeys.
PINOCCHIO	So you brought us here just to make us into donkeys?
COACHMAN	That's right, young feller.
PINOCCHIO	And now you're going to sell us?
COACHMAN	Right again.
CANDLEWICK	Who to?

NOTES

(25) Mimed again, including remarks about each other's freshly grown ears and tails.

COACHMAN	A circus.
PINOCCHIO & CANDLEWICK	A circus? Hooray, that's wonderful. I've always wanted to be in a circus.
COACHMAN	[*a little put out by this enthusiasm*] Maybe you won't be so keen when you get there though. They'll make yer work. Come on the both of you—gee up. Go on, get a move on. Gee up there.

> [*He drives them on a short journey through the auditorium and back towards the stage area. As they approach this:*]

COACHMAN	There y'are. Just ahead of 'ee. There's yer new home. Hulloa there, Circus Master—I brought you a couple of new beasts for the circus.

> [*Enter the* CIRCUS MASTER, *a gaunt looking type.*]

COACHMAN	Here y'are, Circus Master. Two of the best for yer, for only two gold pieces each.
CIRCUS M.	Two gold pieces *each*. Not likely. Not more than one each.
COACHMAN	One! For beasts of this quality. Come, come, sir. I know a good donkey when I see one—and I see two here, and they're two of the best. Four gold pieces is all I ask.
CIRCUS M.	Definitely not four—two.
COACHMAN	Four.
CIRCUS M.	Two.
COACHMAN	Four.
CIRCUS M.	Two.
COACHMAN	All right—I'll drop it a bit. Three and a half.
CIRCUS M.	No. Definitely not more than two and a half.
COACHMAN	Three and a half.
CIRCUS M.	Two and a half.
COACHMAN	Three and a half.
CIRCUS M.	Two and a half.
BOTH	Oh, all right—THREE.

> [*They shake hands, compliment one another on the bargain, and the satisfied* COACHMAN *departs with his coach and horses.*]

CIRCUS M.	[*kind but firm*] Now, you two. It's very nice to 'ave you 'ere in the circus. You work 'ard and you'll 'ave a good time 'ere, with plenty of good straw and grass to eat. I want you to appear in tonight's performance, so we'd better get to work straight away. Ahoy, out there. One of you people bring me in a hoop. D'you 'ear—a hoop for the donkeys.

> [*The* TIGHT-ROPE WALKER (*the Fairy again*) *brings a hoop.*]

CIRCUS M.	Hello. You're new 'ere, aren't you?

TIGHT-ROPE WALKER	Yes—I start tonight.
CIRCUS M.	Do you? What do you do?
TIGHT-ROPE WALKER	I'm a Tight-rope walker.
CIRCUS M.	All right. See you later. [*he ignores her and turns to* CANDLE- WICK] Now then—you first—come over here.

[CANDLEWICK *goes to him, and while he tries to get* CANDLEWICK *into the right position, the* TIGHT- ROPE WALKER *bends quickly down to* PINOCCHIO.]

TIGHT-ROPE WALKER	[*whispering*] I've found your Pop—sssh—don't say a word. Just listen, and do what I tell you. During the performance tonight you must both escape. Wait for my turn, and as soon as I start walking along the tight-rope, run for it. Tell your friend to go up into the hills and wait there. You run down to the sea and start swimming. Understand?
PINOCCHIO	Yes, I understand. How's Pop?
TIGHT-ROPE WALKER	I couldn't speak to him—but I know where he is.
CIRCUS M.	[*to* TIGHT-ROPE WALKER] What d'you think you're doing. Let that donkey alone and go about your business.
TIGHT-ROPE WALKER	I was only. . . .
CIRCUS M.	I don't care what you were only. Go away, we've got work to do. [*exit* TIGHT-ROPE WALKER] Now come on you, etc., etc.

[*The actual dialogue during the 'training scene' will depend on what tricks it is decided to include and can be worked out during rehearsals. (26) When all is done—*]

CIRCUS M.	Not bad. Not bad at all. You do it like that this evening and the crowd'll be very pleased with you—and so shall I. Now I've got to go and see to one or two other new turns. So you have a rest and I'll come for you when the procession starts.

[*He goes out, leaving the donkeys together. As soon as he is out of sight,* PINOCCHIO *starts jumping for joy all over the place.* CANDLEWICK *sits miserable, watching him.*]

NOTES

(26) It should be borne in mind that the donkey act will not be done in the circus performance that night, so some measure of achievement should be reached during the training.

CANDLEWICK   Can't see what there is to dance about.
PINOCCHIO   Ah. You didn't hear what the Tight-rope walker said.
CANDLEWICK   What?
PINOCCHIO   She says that my Pop's all right, and that during tonight's
             performance we must wait for her turn and as soon
             as she starts we're to make a bolt for it. You're to
             go up into the hills and stay there—and I'm to go
             down to the sea and start swimming.
CANDLEWICK   Swimming? Where to?
             [*The Drums, etc., start for the procession.*]
PINOCCHIO   Well, there's no time to talk about it now. Will you do
             it—just as I said?
CANDLEWICK   Yes—course I will.
PINOCCHIO   Good. Here they come.
             [*The procession comes from and crosses back of stage
             area, going up one far side of the auditorium. It
             consists of the drummer (CIRCUS MASTER), CLOWNS,
             ACROBATS, a SNAKE CHARMER—and the TIGHT-
             ROPE WALKER, who fetches the two DONKEYS. There
             is music as well as drumming, and as the procession
             'winds through the streets' the clowns and acrobats—
             and perhaps the others too—entertain the crowds to
             encourage them to attend the circus. The procession
             finishes up at the back of the stage area, with the
             CIRCUS MASTER on the stage, disengaging himself
             from the drum. He announces his circus in real circus
             style.*] (27)
CIRCUS M.   Ladies and Gentlemen. Tonight you are about to see the
             greatest living show on earth—a show of fun and
             daring and spectacle, the like of which has never
             been seen before. It's stupendous, colossal, and
             worth every penny you pay to see it. And tonight
             it's my pleasure to introduce to you first 'Hey
             Presto' the Clown, and 'Press Hey Ho' the Acrobat.
             Music.
             [*And through the music the CLOWN and ACROBAT do
             their stuff for the delight of all and then run off.*]
CIRCUS M.   And now, Ladies and Gentlemen, one of the most
             amazing women in the world—Flatinga, the Snake
             Charmer, who makes pets of the world's deadliest
             snakes——
             [*There is Eastern music and FLATINGA either enters
             or is discovered sitting with a charming collection of
             snakes, with whom she does things—and leaves.*]

NOTES

(27) Important to achieve a circus 'ring'. This, of course, will be
easy for those accepting an arena production.

CIRCUS M.   And next, Ladies and Gentlemen, the most daring, the
               most courageous, the most terrific tight-rope
               walker in the whole world. . . .
                    [*The* TIGHT-ROPE WALKER *runs in and bows to the
                    applause, climbs an imaginary ladder—then, in an
                    almost pin-point spot (on the top half of her only),
                    commences her breathtaking walk. Roll of Drums.*]
                    (28)
                    Then behind her we see the shapes of PINOCCHIO *and*
                    CANDLEWICK, *still on all fours—creeping stealthily
                    away from their captors.*]

PINOCCHIO   Run, Candlewick. Run. Run.
                    [*And they both dash for it up the gangways. There is
                    confusion in the Circus—everyone falling over every-
                    one else—and the* TIGHT-ROPE WALKER *successfully
                    misdirecting everyone so that they lose both* CANDLE-
                    WICK *and* PINOCCHIO. *The confused mob disappear.*
                    CANDLEWICK *disappears at the same time.* PINOC-
                    CHIO *is then seen swimming back through the
                    auditorium.*] (29)

NOTES

(28)   It doesn't matter if the lighting effect cannot be achieved. If
       she is breath-taking enough, that is why the donkeys would
       escape unnoticed.
(29)   The audience could supply the noise of winds and waves. The
       volume of this noise can be controlled easily if a record of 'wind
       and waves' is used at the same time.

PINOCCHIO	This is easy—that's the best of being a wooden puppet— you just float as long as you like. Funny though— gosh, here's the bottom. I must be on a sand bank. I wonder if Pop's here. *[From the stage area there looms up a dark shape. It is the monster and it comes to rest centre stage.]*
PINOCCHIO	*[calling]* Pop. Pop.
GEPETTO	*[from inside monster]* Hello. Who's that?
PINOCCHIO	It's me, Pop. Pinocchio.
GEPETTO	Pinocchio? It can't be. Is it? Pinocchio?
PINOCCHIO	Yes, yes, it's me. How did you get in there?
GEPETTO	I rowed in when the monster was asleep. He always sleeps with his mouth open like this. And now that we're stuck on this sand bank he does nothing but sleep.
PINOCCHIO	Then can't you row out again?
GEPETTO	No, the boat's got stuck.
PINOCCHIO	Oh dear. Well, can you get out of the boat?
GEPETTO	Yes, Pinocchio, but that's no use—I can't swim.
PINOCCHIO	That doesn't matter, Pop. I can and I float easily, being made of wood. All you do is to hang on to me. Come on quickly—while he's still asleep. *[GEPETTO leaves the monster.]*
PINOCCHIO	We can't leave the poor monster stuck on the sand bank.
GEPETTO	No, no. That'll never do.
PINOCCHIO	Let's try and push him off, shall we?
GEPETTO	Do you think we can?
PINOCCHIO	Well, let's try anyway. *[They push and they heave and slowly the monster is pushed clear of the bank and makes for the open sea.]* (30)
PINOCCHIO	That's done it. There he goes. Oh, it's good to see you again, Pop. Hang on to me and we'll swim ashore. *[They swim round the auditorium, and back to the stage area where they clamber ashore.]*
PINOCCHIO	Here we are, Pop. Safely ashore. Pooooof!
GEPETTO	Thank you, Pinocchio. You must be very tired now.
PINOCCHIO	No, Pop. Just a bit puffed. But look, Pop—I've got a wonderful surprise for you. *[He holds out the five gold pieces.]*
GEPETTO	What? Oh, Pinocchio, how wonderful. Where did you get them from?

NOTES

(30)   Some of the audience might swim out to the sand bank to help push the monster and then swim back again.

PINOCCHIO	Mr Fire-Eater sent them because I taught his puppets to work without strings—and he wants you to make some puppets for him as soon as you get home. So you'll have a job again.
	[*During this we hear the Puppet Theatre Company's music (procession) getting nearer.*]
PINOCCHIO	Listen. There's Mr Fire-Eater now. They must be coming for the big show.
	[*And with the music getting louder and louder, the puppet company arrives. There are greetings all round, particularly between* FIRE-EATER *and* GEPETTO. *Then* FIRE-EATER *notices his son,* CANDLEWICK, *who has wandered down from the hills during the greetings.*]
FIRE-EATER	My dear boy—what has happened to you?
CANDLEWICK	I don't know exactly, father.
FIRE-EATER	But this is terrible.
CANDLEWICK	It's my own fault really. I was a silly ass and wanted to go to the Land of the Boobies instead of to school—and when I got there, I *was* a silly ass. I'm terribly sorry about it.
FIRE-EATER	Oh dear. Is there nothing we can do? [*pause*] Can no one think of anything?
	[*There is a moment's silence, and then:*]
GEPETTO	Yes, by all the stars, there is something we can do.
FIRE-EATER	What? Anything? I'll do anything.
GEPETTO	Then just stand quite still everyone.
	[*Quietly,* GEPETTO *wishes by himself. As at the start of the play, there is again the sound of 'charmingly eerie music'. The* FAIRY *arrives, now her own beautiful self again.*] (31)
FAIRY	Who calls me?
	[*There is no answer—and she walks slowly down the stage and gently touches* GEPETTO.]
GEPETTO	Oh, it *is* you. You've come again. I thought we'd bothered you so much lately that perhaps you wouldn't want to come any more.
FAIRY	I'm always glad to come. Is it about Pinocchio again?
GEPETTO	No, no, not this time.
FAIRY	Where is Pinocchio?
PINOCCHIO	Here I am.
FAIRY	I don't think you know me, do you?

NOTES

(31)   Some audiences might well enjoy wishing again for the Fairy, but with others this will not hold at this stage of the play. Only Gepetto can tell at the moment it is due to happen—and he must act accordingly.

PINOCCHIO	Well, I'm not sure. You remind me of someone I once met—in fact several people.
FAIRY	Who are they?
PINOCCHIO	Oh, there's a cricket, and a frog, and a bird—even a tight-rope walker. Do you know them? [*The* FAIRY *whispers in his ear.*] Really? Were you? Gosh! (32)
FAIRY	Sssh. Keep it a secret. Now, Mr Gepetto, what can I do for you this time?
GEPETTO	Well, my friend Mr Fire-Eater here, has a donkey called Candlewick—only he shouldn't be a donkey at all.
FAIRY	Shouldn't he? Then we must do something about it. Candlewick, come here. Now go to the well and pour water over your head. [*With everyone crowding round,* CANDLEWICK *puts his head in the well. When he withdraws it, the ears have gone—and he is able to stand upright as a boy again.*]
PINOCCHIO	[*to* CANDLEWICK] Now what about Magic, eh?
CANDLEWICK	It's incredible. I can't believe it.
FIRE-EATER	Madam, how can I ever thank you. Would you be so kind as to stay as our guest to see the puppet show we are about to perform. The only stringless puppets in the. . . .
FAIRY	Thank you, Mr Fire-Eater. I should love it. [FIRE-EATER *calls for everyone to get ready for the great show. There is much bustle and excitement, including an invitation to* GEPETTO *and* PINOCCHIO, *to take part in the show. They accept, and* FIRE-EATER *presents his show.*]
FIRE-EATER	Ladies and Gentlemen, Boys and Girls, you are now about to see the only stringless puppets in the world in their great performance of 'The Harlequinade'. [*He then drops the showmanship a little, and, rather on the lines of the Stage Manager in 'Our Town', sets the picture and the situation and the characters of the play. As he speaks of the characters, so do we see them—but they are quite absorbed in their own world, so that we see them without fuss and bother.* HARLEQUIN *enters, and makes for the* FIRE-EATER'S *house.* *The introduction might be something as follows.* (33)

NOTES

(32) With some audiences, Pinocchio might whisper out to them— 'Did *you* know?'

(33) With some audiences, there would be no need for any introduction at all.

FIRE-EATER   That is Harlequin, and he lives in that house over there. He loves a maiden who lives on the other side of the street—there she is now—with her father, Pantalone, who for some reason won't hear of his daughter marrying Harlequin. But Columbine has a maid who takes letters to Harlequin and arranges meeting places for them when her father's busy. Well, busy isn't quite the word, because he spends most of his time eating sausages, which this butcher boy delivers from his shop just down the road there. But there is no need for me to tell you any more of the story because, though nobody in the play says a word, yet the story speaks for itself.

[*There follows a performance of the Harlequinade, which the* FAIRY *watches from the audience. When it is over, and the applause has died down, the* FAIRY *goes back to the stage.*]

FAIRY   Thank you, Mr Fire-Eater. It was lovely. And now, before I go, there is one thing I have to do here. Mr Gepetto.

GEPETTO   Yes.

FAIRY   Do you remember what I asked you soon after you had made Pinocchio? Do you?

GEPETTO   You asked me if I would like him to be a real boy.

FAIRY   And would you?

GEPETTO   Yes, yes. I would.

FAIRY   And what about you, Pinocchio? Would you like to be a boy?

PINOCCHIO   Yes, yes, I think I would. I mean—well, it's a bit silly a puppet going to school, isn't it? I mean I never seem to get there as a puppet. If I was a boy, perhaps I would.

FAIRY   Very well, then. But you must help me, Pinocchio. Now —stand quite still and concentrate very, very hard.

[*He does so, and, in front of our very eyes, the stiffness goes out of* PINOCCHIO *and he changes from a puppet to a boy. Everyone is astonished. Everyone is happy. (The dialogue for this climax should be built up at rehearsals, through improvisation.)* (34) *And when the commotion and the wonderings are over, they turn to look for the* FAIRY *to thank her. But she has gone. . .*]

GEPETTO   And I did so want to thank her.

PINOCCHIO   Listen!

[*From the distance comes the sound of the* FAIRY'S *music. And also in the distance the* FAIRY'S *voice, floating through space.*]

FAIRY   Good-bye, Mr Gepetto. Good-bye, Pinocchio. And if ever you need me again, you know how to call me. . . .

[*They wave good-bye to the air, rather sadly. And the spell is broken by the practical* FIRE-EATER.]

FIRE-EATER   Come along everyone. There's work to be done. Form up the procession—for all the world waits to see Fire-Eater's amazing stringless puppets.

[*The big drum strikes up. Music follows. The procession forms, and marches away to the back of the stage area.*

There are no curtain calls as such. Instead the procession comes back and marches through the audience, waving and calling goodnight and good-bye, and then walks all round the theatre until, as it started, it fades away in the distance.] (35)

END

NOTES

(34)   Indeed the whole climax can be adapted to the needs and experience of the group. For instance, it would be possible for the Fairy to ask the audience to suggest the magic words that will help the 'transformation'; when she is satisfied she has the right words she could then ask the audience to repeat them over and over, *in a whisper*, until the change is complete.

Beware of comedy of the wrong kind creeping in. This is the climax of the whole play.

(35)   Or perhaps the audience joins on to the end of the procession and in this manner is led out of the 'theatre'.

GENERAL NOTES

Costumes: Try to have them really gay and colourful. Although they can (and should) be based on *Commedia del Arte*, they should be simple. The wearers must be able to move about very easily.

Scenery: Anything the company or group likes. Except—set scenes that require changing, which would not only be most out of style but would slow up the production. It is perhaps best to have no scenery, or merely curtains and skycloth with cut-outs (the original setting by Richard Lake had a brilliant blue skycloth in front of which was a composite building—Gepetto's house, a platform, and the puppet workshop, with upper level and a flagpole for people to slide down.) The fun and the value is in designing your own setting.

Music: Improvise where you can. Keep the School or Amateur Music Society out unless they can really enter into the spirit of the play. Where 'real' music is needed have good recordings—for the rest improvise with percussion, and whatever you can muster.

Suggestions:

For Processions—any favourite march.

The 'charmingly eerie music'—a phrase of the suite 'Daphnis and Chloé' (Ravel).

The Harlequinade, etc.—'Mam'selle Angot' (Lecoq, arr. Jacob).

When the Puppets learn to dance—'Little Rock-Get-Away' (Les Paul, played on Swing Guitar).

The music *must* be light and gay.